Hannelore B. and Rudolph B. SCHULHOF COLLECTION

Hannelore B. and Rudolph B.
SCHULHOF

COLLECTION

Edited by

Philip Rylands

Essay by

Nicholas Fox Weber

Interview by

Lisa Jacobs

Photography by

David Heald

GUGGENHEIM

Hannelore B. and Rudolph B. Schulhof Collection

ISBN: 978-0-89207-417-4

Guggenheim Museum Publications
1071 Fifth Avenue
New York, New York 10128
www.guggenheim.org

Peggy Guggenheim Collection
Palazzo Venier dei Leoni
Dorsoduro 701
I-30123 Venezia
www.guggenheim-venice.it

Design: Don Quaintance, Public Address Design
Design and production assistant: Elizabeth Frizzell
Production: Suzana Greene, Melissa Secondino
Editorial: Elizabeth Franzen, Jennifer Knox White
Typography: Locator (display) and Stempel Schneidler (text)

Cover: Eduardo Chillida, *Stele for Millares (Estela a Millares)*, 1960–72. Steel, 174 x 160 x 125 cm. Solomon R. Guggenheim Foundation, New York, Hannelore B. and Rudolph B. Schulhof Collection, promised gift of Hannelore B. Schulhof

Frontispiece: Sol LeWitt, *Incomplete Open Cube 6/8*, 1974. Painted aluminum, 106.7 x 106.7 x 106.7 cm. Solomon R. Guggenheim Foundation, New York, Hannelore B. and Rudolph B. Schulhof Collection, promised gift of Hannelore B. Schulhof

Printed in Germany by GZD

Contents

This book celebrates the outstanding collection of postwar and contemporary European and American art assembled over the course of five decades by two visionary collectors. The paintings, sculptures, and works on paper presented here, from the Hannelore B. and Rudolph B. Schulhof Collection, have been promised as a gift to the Solomon R. Guggenheim Foundation, to be housed in the Peggy Guggenheim Collection.

Hannelore Schulhof and her husband, Rudolph Schulhof (1912–1999), arrived in New York from Europe in 1940. (They had first met in Prague but had lived most recently in Belgium.) They began collecting art in the late 1940s, and by the 1980s had acquired a reputation for the refinement of their choices and the care with which their works were selected. They frequently developed friendships with the artists whose work they acquired. The Schulhofs' collection is exemplary of the truism that fine collections are built from connoisseurship and passion. Altruism and philanthropy also define their relationship to art. The Schulhofs served on the boards and committees of numerous arts organizations, including the National Gallery of Art, Brooklyn Museum, and Whitney Museum of American Art. In 1965 Rudolph was a founding director of the Israel Museum in Jerusalem, and for more than three decades he and Hannelore generously supported this museum with endowment funds and gifts of art. In 1980 Hannelore and Rudolph both became charter members of the Advisory Board of the Peggy Guggenheim Collection; Hannelore would become a lifetime emeritus member, while from 1994 to 1998 Rudolph would serve on the Board of Trustees of the Solomon R. Guggenheim Foundation. Hannelore has also served as a board member of the International Council of Museums (ICOM) and as a founding member and financial supporter of ICOM's International Committee for Museums and Collections of Modern Art (CIMAM). She joined the Board of Trustees of the American Federation of Arts in 1981 and served for many years as the board's vice president and as chair from 2004 to 2005.

The Solomon R. Guggenheim Foundation is in large part a collection of collections, conserving in its holdings major contributions to the history of collecting in the twentieth century, including those of Solomon R. Guggenheim himself, his art advisor (and the first director of the museum that bears his name) Hilla Rebay, the art dealer Karl Nierendorf, Justin K. and Hilde Thannhauser, Katherine Dreier, Solomon's niece Peggy Guggenheim, and, more recently, Count Giuseppe Panza di Biumo, The Robert Mapplethorpe Foundation, and The Bohen Foundation. We are honored and grateful that, with this promised gift, we will welcome Hannelore and Rudolph Schulhof into this circle of distinguished collectors and generous benefactors.

We would like to thank Lisa Jacobs, Curator of the Hannelore B. and Rudolph B. Schulhof Collection, for her invaluable contributions to this publication, among them the recollections by Hannelore Schulhof she has brought together in these pages. Ms. Jacobs also worked closely with David Heald, Director of Photographic Services and Chief Photographer, Guggenheim Museum, as he photographed the collection to which she is so dedicated. We are grateful to Mr. Heald, a veteran maker of fine photographs of fine art, for creating an intimate record of the collection as the Schulhofs experienced it, surrounding them in their Manhattan and Long Island homes. We thank author and biographer Nicholas Fox Weber for his essay, and Don Quaintance, of Public Address Design, whose genius for book design has benefited this catalogue immensely. We are grateful to Ana Debenedetti, Jared Quinton, Simone Rutkowitz, and Susan Thompson for their work on the artists' biographies, to Chiara Barbieri, Director of Publications and Special Projects, Peggy Guggenheim Collection; Simone Bottazzin, Publications Assistant, Peggy Guggenheim Collection; Elizabeth Franzen, Associate Director of Publications, Editorial, Guggenheim Museum; Suzana Greene, Production Associate, Guggenheim Museum; Giulia Mazzolani, Assistant to the Director, Peggy Guggenheim Collection; and Melissa Secondino, Associate Director of Publications, Production, Guggenheim Museum, for their professionalism, and especially to Jennifer Knox White for her editorial work. Thank you to Susan Davidson, Senior Curator, Collections & Exhibitions, Guggenheim Museum, and to Elizabeth Levy, Director of Publications and Web Site, Guggenheim Museum, for their leadership, good judgment, and experience.

We are grateful to Miles and Nancy Rubin and Michael P. Schulhof for providing funding for this publication. We have benefited from Michael Schulhof's incomparable counsel, goodwill, and encouragement in bringing this enterprise to conclusion. In the context of the promised gift of these works, we also thank Art System (Venice), Alberto Bisello, Monica Ceravolo, Lisa Jacobs, Alessandra Bonetti Rubelli, Stanley Schlesinger, Jr., and Maurizio Torcellan.

We offer our sincere appreciation to the Schulhof family. Above all, we honor the memory of Rudolph Schulhof and thank Hannelore Schulhof, by whose permission this book is published and who will one day generously entrust the works pictured here to the Peggy Guggenheim Collection of the Solomon R. Guggenheim Foundation.

Richard Armstrong
Director, Solomon R. Guggenheim Museum and Foundation

Philip Rylands
Director, Peggy Guggenheim Collection

SCHULHOF COLLECTION Story

Astute and Refined The Schulhofs' Discerning Vision

NICHOLAS FOX WEBER

The art acquired with intense determination and remarkable passion by Hannelore and Rudolph Schulhof over the course of half a century is almost entirely abstract. Yet, while it does not represent familiar imagery, it has the titanic force of nature at its most powerful. The Schulhofs' collection reflects and elicits intense human feeling.

This is by no means the side of abstraction used to express the unconscious. It is, rather, abstraction based on steely control, its rigor allowing it to impart powerful emotions to the viewer. Feelings ranging from a soothing and distant calm to a kettle-drum triumph, from clear resolution to mysterious complexity, come from the forms and materials. These qualities do not derive from the private experiences of the painters and sculptors who created this remarkable work, but from their restraint and engagement. For its vast variety, the Schulhofs' collection is unified by the intelligence and palpable honesty of the artists who made the work, and of the people who put it together.

Hannelore Schulhof refers to the unifying element of her taste as "minimalism."[1] True, but this is minimalism with maximum impact. Where there is reduction, as indeed there is in so many of these works, the paring down gives the object a life of its own. The work, consistently, is profoundly human, as emotive as ancient ruins, ineffably rich behind the apparent leanness. What is simple has been packed and tightened to have the hard core of a meteor, and what is quiet has the silence of an emperor: the deliberate quietude that signifies ultimate power. The art, in short, has some of the same attributes as the people who collected it: a no-nonsense astuteness, a refinement, and a prudence grounded on the experience of some of the toughest vicissitudes and vagaries the human experience can offer. The

bold sculptures of Eduardo Chillida, the quintessential paintings of Ellsworth Kelly
and Kenneth Noland in their formative years, the stirring reductionism of Donald
Judd, the poetic quietude of Robert Ryman: these all manifest the courage, the grasp
of what is true and solid after a struggle to get there, the embrace of wonder that
offers certitude and confidence, that are true ballast to life's discomfiting situations.

Hannelore Schulhof does not dissemble about the realities of her and her husband's lives. Speaking with the octogenarian collector, one learns of a glamorous
youth cut short by the rise of Nazism. Hannelore Buck Schulhof spent her early
childhood in Berlin, in happy circumstances. Her main memory is of playing marbles,
she told me in response to my suggestion that she might have looked at art as a
little girl. The insistence that she was just a kid who liked having a good time is
clear. Yet, at the same time, that someone so attached to sculpture, so aware of the
beauty of perfect forms and the pleasures of the tactile experience of stone, should
come up with "playing marbles" as her instant association is telling, as it conforms
completely to the tastes that would later take such sophisticated form in her attrac-
tion to strong materials, to objects in motion, and to the impeccable execution of
craft of all types.

When the Buck family moved to Vienna in the mid-1930s—Hannelore's father,
in the postcard-publishing business, had offices in many Eastern European cities—
she had a "great time," her strongest memory being of attending balls. That all began
to change one weekend in 1937 when her father persuaded her mother, reluctant
to make the journey, to take the train to Prague for what was intended to be a long
weekend. A few hours after the entire Buck family had pulled out of the railroad
station, Hitler's troops marched into Austria. Being Jewish, the Bucks had left just
in time.

From Prague, the publisher and his wife and daughters moved to Brussels.
Mr. Buck decided to send Hannelore to London to learn English. There she encoun-
tered, for a second time, Rudolph Schulhof, ten years her senior. They had met

previously in Prague, on a blind date; Rudolph had been "furious," at the time, to have been conned by his brother, who lived in the same building as Hannelore's sister, into breaking a date with another young woman to go out with Hannelore. Chaperones had been in attendance, and it had been awkward, but what may have been less than entertaining at the time gains charm in the retelling, for Hannelore Schulhof's reminiscences have the wry humor, the sense of "this is how it was, simply and inarguably," that is essential to everything about the collector and so consistent with the candor of the art she prefers.

At their second meeting, Rudolph was in London for business, and again they had tea—although this time without chaperones. Shortly thereafter, in 1940, they were married in her parents' home in Brussels. One has little doubt that the evaluation of their son Michael (Mickey) that his mother was "an intellectually mature seventeen" at the time is on the mark.[2]

The newlyweds headed to Spa, a resort in the Ardennes known for its mineral springs, for their honeymoon. Some twenty years later, in Palm Beach, Florida, Rudolph Schulhof discovered while reading William Shirer's *Rise and Fall of the Third Reich* that Hitler had planned to invade Belgium and would have swept through Spa en route to Brussels at the precise moment they were there. Hannelore, with her impeccable and unequivocal grasp of the facts of this detail of history, explained that the Führer changed his plans because a reconnaissance plane had been shot down and he was afraid that spies had discovered his army's intentions. When Rudolph learned about their fortunate escape—not unlike that of Hannelore's family when they departed Vienna for Prague—he was so shaken that he awakened his wife in the middle of the night. How appropriate it was that the Schulhofs were in Palm Beach to celebrate the Jewish holiday of Passover—which commemorates

Fig. 3
Rudolph Schulhof, 1972

Fig. 4
Hannelore Schulhof, Delos, Greece, 1958

Fig. 5
Afro (left) with Hannelore and Rudolph Schulhof, Rome, 1957

Fig. 6
Giuseppe Santomaso (center) with Hannelore and Rudolph Schulhof, Peggy Guggenheim Collection, Venice, 1982

another miraculous escape—and that so many years later Hannelore, in a beautiful house with marvelous art in every direction, should have such utter clarity in recalling the harsh realities that have accompanied her good fortune.

The young couple's existence was to get tougher before it got easier. In 1940 Hannelore and her parents were able to get immigration visas in time to board the *Rex*, the last ship out of Europe, but Rudolph had no visa and remained behind. For a time the young bride wondered whether her husband would ever get into the United States. Fortunately, he was able to do so shortly after, having received a visa first from Canada.

And so their life in New York began. Rudolph Schulhof had gone into his father-in-law's publishing company, producing art reproductions and greeting cards, with the bulk of his business devoted to Catholic greeting cards used as fundraising materials by archdioceses all over the United States. The family had fled Europe with the color-separated film and plates essential to the production of these cards. By 1947 Hannelore and Rudolph Schulhof had three small sons and sufficient means to leave their small apartment in the Washington Heights neighborhood of Manhattan and move to Kings Point, in the Great Neck area on the north shore of Long Island. By 1952, the year when their daughter was born, the family business had become sufficiently established to enable Rudolph to open an office in Milan in order to buy art to reproduce on the greeting cards and to get good supplies for color separations.

He and Hannelore also began to look at art of a very different sort. In Great Neck, they met people who collected work by the sculptor Chaim Gross and by Raphael and Moses Soyer. The Schulhofs' tastes, however, quickly went in other directions. They absorbed exciting things, and a few circumstances converged that turned them into collectors of international contemporary art. For one thing, they attended the Artists' Equity Ball and became aware of the reality of the lives of the struggling creators the event supported. For another, they went to see the great art dealer Justin Thannhauser to buy a gift for Hannelore. They had settled on a Rouault, but Rudolph then realized he could not afford it. The young businessman attempted to get the gallery owner to lower his price, only to have Thannhauser advise them, "Look at the art of your own time."

They followed that advice. When Rudolph was in Milan working on color separations, his wife was off at the galleries, discovering artists like Afro and Alberto Burri. Hannelore had taken an art history course in Belgium and attended classes at the Museum of Modern Art in New York, but what interested her was not just the work being done in her own time but also the possibility of meeting its makers. The Schulhofs befriended Burri, who lived north of Milan, and who intrigued them in spite of, or perhaps because of, his "explosive" personality. They also became close to Afro, and to the artist Giuseppe Santomaso. Soon enough, they were, without fail, attending Documenta and the Venice Biennale.

In 1954, on one of those trips to the Biennale, they were going through Peggy Guggenheim's palazzo on a day when the collection was open to the public. The doyenne of the house heard the young couple debating whether or not a work was

by Santomaso. "Yes, it's a Santomaso," announced the collector, whom Hannelore Schulhof instantly recognized as the person she had seen in her private gondola going down the Grand Canal. That conversation was the beginning of the friendship that would, some forty years later, lead to the plans for so many of the Schulhofs' works to go to Venice to be housed in their own gallery and sculpture garden within the Peggy Guggenheim Collection.

The presence of Alexander Calder's work at the Peggy Guggenheim Collection has long been one of its strengths. Now, with the addition of three stupendous Calders from the Schulhofs' collection, the Calder holdings in Venice present the innovator of moving sculpture so that his existential force and unparalleled wit exist in tandem.

To be underneath the 1966 *Yellow Moon* is to have an experience that perfectly conjures Jean-Paul Sartre's essay on the American sculptor. The French philosopher wrote:

> A mobile, one might say, is a little private celebration, an object defined by its movement and having no other existence. It is a flower that fades when it ceases to move, a pure play of movement in the sense that we speak of a pure play of light. . . .
>
> A mobile does not suggest anything: it captures genuine living moments and shapes them. Mobiles have no meaning, make you think of nothing but themselves. They are, that is all; they are absolutes. There is no more of the unpredictable about them than in any other human creation. No human brain, not even their creator's, could possibly see all the complex combinations of which they are capable. A general destiny of movement is sketched for them, and then they are left to work it out for themselves.[3]

Fig. 8

Alexander Calder's *Yellow Moon* (1966) in the sunroom
of the Schulhofs' Kings Point residence, 2010

In many ways, this is the experience offered by much of the art in the Schulhofs'
collection. To look for extraneous meaning in these works is to miss the point; to
accept, and marvel at, the presence of the absolute, is to know the rewards of the
artists' bravery and imagination.

Sartre continues, "Valéry said of the sea that it is perpetual recommencement.
A mobile is in this way like the sea, and is equally enchanting: forever rebeginning,
forever new. No use throwing it a passing glance, you must live with it and be
fascinated by it."[4] This sentiment, so perfectly applicable to the Schulhofs' Calders,
pertains to much else dear to them as well. The art to which they instinctively
gravitated is work that merits contemplation; it is work that will make its imprint
on you over time. Like the people who acquired these forceful objects initially and
lived with them in their home, the viewer who sees them in their museum setting
should take time, remain passive before them, and allow their charming and mag-
isterial aspects to unfold.

Sartre goes on to describe a wonderful event:

I was talking with Calder one day in his studio when suddenly a mobile beside
me, which until then had been quiet, became violently agitated. I stepped
quickly back, thinking to be out of its reach. But then, when the agitation had
ceased and it appeared to have relapsed into quiescence, its long majestic tail,

which until then had not budged, began mournfully to wave and, sweeping through the air, brushed across my face. These hesitations, resumptions, gropings, clumsinesses, the sudden decisions and above all the swan-like grace make of certain mobiles very strange creatures indeed, something between matter and life.

In short, although mobiles do not seek to imitate anything...they are nevertheless at once lyrical inventions, technical combinations of an almost mathematical quality and sensitive symbols of Nature.[5]

What occurred to the philosopher can readily be echoed for the perceptive viewer of *Yellow Moon*. The principles apply to much that is encompassed in the Schulhofs' vision of other artists as well. Above all, there is that realm "between matter and life." And there is the combination of the mathematical and the natural. You are in the territory of pure art, of art that is referential to much in one's knowledge of other domains, but something entirely its own. It has taken the most discerning eyes, the most original and willing approach to looking and seeing, to bring all this together.

Mickey Schulhof succinctly explains his parents' lifelong collecting policy: "If you're going to acquire art, buy it from artists you know. You get to understand a body of work, not just a single piece, and you get to know someone interesting." One might add: "If you're going to acquire a work from a source other than the artist, buy it from a gallerist who knows the artist well." Hannelore and Rudolph Schulhof were not interested in amassing individual pieces as trophies; rather, they pursued work by the painters and sculptors they most admired, and collected it in depth. They kept every piece they acquired, never selling a thing. Having started with smaller works, when they moved to a larger house with capacious grounds, they branched out into impressive outdoor pieces. As a result, their collection

Fig. 9
Hannelore Schulhof with her son and daughter-in-law, Michael and Paola Schulhof, at the Solomon R. Guggenheim Museum, New York, September 15, 2010

includes both small and large works by Calder, Marino Marini, and others of their favorites. Art became the family religion, a source of intense spiritual satisfaction and an integral part of the children's upbringings.

Some of the couple's acquaintances with artists were cursory, some very close. The collectors met Calder, Marini, Joan Miró, and the other older and well-known artists whose work they acquired; they became especially close to Pol Bury (even holding his wedding at their house) and to Louise Nevelson. They traveled around the Basque Country with Chillida. Their friendships, their acumen, their constant gallery-going, their endless studying of catalogues and books, and their frequent visits to museums enabled them to be connoisseurs in the truest sense. Their son remarks, "When they chose a work, they knew all of the artist's work at the time; they knew where the piece fit in." This, surely, is why so many of the works by the Minimalist painters and sculptors in their collection show these artists at their seminal moments; the force of discovery emanates from the pieces the Schulhofs acquired. Buying Chillida sculptures directly from their maker's studio in San Sebastián, the Schulhofs gravitated to the gems; selecting an early Kenneth Noland "target" painting, they fastened on to the remarkable 1961 *Birth* (originally given by the artist to Clement Greenberg to celebrate the birth of Greenberg's child). By going to the Biennale and to Documenta time and again, by visiting and revisiting artists' studios, by working with only a few gallery owners, they honed their knowledge and their eye, and as a result were able to select not just any works by Lucio Fontana, but two of the richest, replete in Fontana's unique qualities of stasis and action and his rare marriage of destruction and aesthetic refinement.

Fig. 10
Pol Bury (center) with Rudolph and Hannelore Schulhof at Bury's wedding in the Schulhofs' garden, Kings Point, New York, April 22, 1970

The Schulhofs rarely bought a work on which they did not agree. Each made
the other return at least one object before the purchase had been finalized—at one
point Rudolph could not live with a Barnett Newman that Hannelore had acquired,
while she felt uncomfortable with a work by Willem de Kooning—but disagree-
ments were rare. Generally, their relationships with the objects they owned were
personal and intense. One feels the profound connection between Hannelore
Schulhof and a vibrant yellow Fontana with holes in it, or the way the unusual
history of a Chillida sculpture—it was "abducted," she explains, on the way to a
museum exhibition in Zurich in 1969 and only reemerged in a small town in Italy
seventeen years later—has become a part of her life. Their John Chamberlain is a
jewel to her, the dealer Leo Castelli having found it when she said that the sculptor
had never made anything small enough for her to be able to house inside. She is
personally thrilled by most of the work in the collection, and certainly would not
have it otherwise.

In 1960 Meyer Schapiro wrote an essay entitled "On the Humanity of Abstract
Painting." After charting the development from representation to abstraction, the
great art historian remarked, "Humanity in art is therefore not confined to the
image of man. Man shows himself too in relation to the surroundings, in his arti-
facts, and in the expressive character of all the signs and marks he produces. These
may be noble or ignoble, playful or tragic, passionate or serene. Or they may be
sensed as unnameable yet compelling moods."[6] Reading those words, one can
readily picture the Schulhofs' small Chillidas, so riveting and dramatic while the
source of their emotions remains elusive, or the Agnes Martin canvases, which
manage the miracle of allowing the playful and tragic to coexist in perfect tandem.

Schapiro's illuminations continue: "It is the painter's constructive ability, his power of impressing a work with feeling and the qualities of thought that gives humanity to art; and this humanity may be realized with an unlimited range of themes or elements of form."[7] One thinks here of the works by Julius Bissier and Cy Twombly in the Schulhofs' collection, and of their revolutionary 1957 canvas by Giuseppe Capogrossi, a perfect example of the collectors' courage to acquire work by an artist known to few Americans, to buy outside the ranks of "blue chip" artists sanctified by auction houses. The Milanese artist's painting has something reptilian to it, an anthropomorphic aspect that recalls pre-Columbian sculpture, a true primordial force. The Schulhofs' Fontanas are similarly strong, as are the works by Jean Dubuffet, so closely connected to the realities of quotidian life. These works, with their rare combination of earthiness and elegance, well suit the woman whose eye found them. They are completely grounded, without an iota of falseness, and have some of the force and bravery of the collector—the beautiful toughness of someone who remembers hardship precisely as she savors luxury, who embraces beauty just as she acknowledges its violations.

When Schapiro wrote his essay, he was on the defensive. That posture is understandable, given the date of his writing. "The charge of inhumanity brought against abstract painting springs from a failure to see the works as they are," he wrote. "They have been obscured by concepts from other fields."[8] It was in that same period that the Schulhofs took their place in the vanguard, selecting artworks with humanity and integrity, with pure strength, while most of their cohorts were attached to a taste for the lyrical and predictable. Moreover, the Schulhofs had made the decision to buy only works by living artists—by people they could know, and hence truly help. As it happens, Schapiro's essay provides a perfect guidepost to their collection. Of work by the pioneering abstractionists, Schapiro writes, "These elementary shapes have a physiognomy; they are live expressive forms. The perfection of the sphere is not only a mathematical insight, we feel its subtle appearance of the centered and evenly rounded as a fulfillment of our need for completeness, concentration, and repose."[9] That visual experience and the resultant emotions hit the nail on the head for the Schulhofs' Franz Kline—a small piece yet one of strong impact—and the ravishing early wall sculpture by Donald Judd, which shows the artist at his moment of discovery, when his gifts for stillness and a sheer, inexplicable visual beauty were at their apogee.

And then, as if he had set out to describe the Schulhofs' superb works by Burri and Martin's *Rose* (1966), Schapiro writes, referring to the American poet Walt Whitman,

> Whitman's description of God as a square depends on his intense vision of the square as a live form:

> Chanting the square deific, out of the One advancing, out of the sides;
> Out of the old and new—out of the square entirely divine,
> Solid, four-sided, (all the sides needed) ... from this side JEHOVAH am I.[10]

Fig. 12

Hannelore and Rudolph Schulhof in their Manhattan residence, 1958

That the attitudes of these paintings' creators emerge is guaranteed by the company the works by Burri and Martin keep in this collection: those abstract squares are flanked by art that primes the viewer to respond to their architectonic power and the ancient yet modern subtleties with which the perfect abstract forms move in and out, invoke motion, and invite the viewer into their private universes.

Schapiro continues to reflect on the power of the square, a form seminal also to the Schulhofs' works by Frank Stella and Carl Andre: "The same form occurred to Tolstoy in his *Diary of a Madman* as an image of religious anguish: 'Something was trying to tear my soul asunder but could not do so. . . . Always the same terror was there—red, white, square. Something is being torn and will not tear.'"[11] Tolstoy's words bring us again to the Schulhofs' Fontanas, for, even though they are not square, the force of these works indeed exists in this simultaneity: they are torn but will not tear.

Gutsy collectors who went to the depths of their own experience in their choices and their tenacity, Rudolph and Hannelore Schulhof time and again pursued artists whose works they knew in unusual depth and were attracted to what was enthralling in just this way. There is never anything flimsy or overrefined in their choices; nothing is just surface. Rather, the refinement is of the truest sort,

Fig. 13
Ellsworth Kelly, *Black Curve IV*, 1972. Oil on canvas,
87.9 x 104.5 cm. Solomon R. Guggenheim Foundation,
New York, Hannelore B. and Rudolph B. Schulhof
Collection, promised gift of Hannelore B. Schulhof

resulting in paintings and sculpture that are rock hard, celestial, and dense—even when they move in the wind. With his gift for homing in on the responsiveness to art at its most deeply felt, Schapiro quotes, toward the end of his essay, someone he deliberately leaves unnamed until after the citation: "How does the straight line feel? It feels, as I suppose it looks, straight—a dull thought drawn out endlessly. It is unstraight lines, or many straight and curved lines together, that are eloquent to the touch. They appear and disappear, are now deep, now shallow, now broken off or lengthened or swelling. They rise and sink beneath my fingers, they are full of sudden starts and pauses, and their variety is inexhaustible and wonderful."[12] The author of those words, Schapiro reveals, is Helen Keller. The critic observes, "Her sensitiveness shames us whose open eyes fail to grasp these qualities of form."[13] One could imagine that Keller knew of the sculpture amassed by the Schulhofs when she wrote these words, for in them it is the combination of straight lines, the rich play of form, that is so moving.

Schapiro's essay ends with a reference to the power of abstract art to convey "inner life and the resources of the imagination."[14] What better evidence of that power could there be than Hannelore and Rudolph Schulhof's collection?

NOTES

1. The author met with Hannelore Schulhof on October 22, 2005, while preparing this essay. All quotations from Mrs. Schulhof are from the conversation that took place that day.

2. All quotations from Mickey Schulhof are from a conversation with the author, September 13, 2005.

3. Jean-Paul Sartre, preface to the catalogue for an exhibition at Galerie Louis Carré, Paris, 1946, quoted in Jean Lipman, *Calder's Universe* (New York: Viking Press, 1976), p. 261.

4. Ibid.

5. Ibid.

6. Meyer Schapiro, "On the Humanity of Abstract Painting," in *Mondrian: On the Humanity of Abstract Painting* (New York: George Braziller, 1978), pp. 9–10.

7. Ibid., p. 10.

8. Ibid., p. 11.

9. Ibid., p. 13.

10. Ibid.

11. Ibid., pp. 13–14.

12. Ibid., p. 14.

13. Ibid.

14. Ibid., p. 17.

Schulhof Collection at Home

Photography by DAVID HEALD

Kings Point, New York

Fig. 14
Schulhof residence, Kings Point, New York, 2010

Fig. 15
Dining room, Schulhof residence, Kings Point, New York, 2010

Fig. 16
Dining room, Schulhof residence, Kings Point, New York, 2010

Fig. 17
Foyer, Schulhof residence, Kings Point, New York, 2010

Manhattan

Fig. 18
Study, Schulhof residence, Manhattan, 2010

Fig. 19
Living room, Schulhof residence, Manhattan, 2010

Conversation with Hannelore Schulhof

LISA JACOBS

Art … is what gives my life a dimension beyond the material
world we live in.

—Hannelore Schulhof

From 1947 on, Rudolph and Hannelore Schulhof devoted themselves to assembling
their impressive collection of postwar and contemporary art. Art, to the Schulhofs,
was more than an interest, diversion, or hobby; it was a lifelong pursuit of the
nobler instincts and of humanistic precepts.

    European born, the Schulhofs were cultured, elegant, and sophisticated. I met
them for the first time in 1998, when they were looking for a new curator for
their collection. I remember walking into their elegant apartment on Fifth Avenue for the interview. The apartment was white and pristine, the perfect back-
drop to their collection. Mrs. Schulhof was wearing gold earrings and a pin that
looked like whimsical abstractions of sea creatures with emerald eyes. She told
me they were a gift from Mr. Schulhof, and that he had commissioned the Italian
artist Afro to make them for her. Mr. Schulhof was immensely charming, with
his distinctive Czech accent and pipe in hand, and had a monumental presence;
his smile could light up a room. Together, they were a mesmerizing couple and a
force in the art world. It was an honor to be hired as the curator of their collection.

    The Schulhofs loved the process of collecting art. They took pleasure in going
to galleries, purchasing art, being with artists, and meeting with dealers; they savored
the atmosphere of museums, entertaining in their art-filled home, and talking
about art. Over time their passion evolved from abstraction to Minimalism, to

Fig. 20
Hannelore and Rudolph Schulhof in their Kings Point
residence, September 17, 1973

Fig. 21
Lisa Jacobs in the study of the Schulhofs' Manhattan
residence, 2011

more conceptually oriented work, and their collection reflected this evolution. Each and every acquisition was a collaboration. Mrs. Schulhof has often told me, "It was a real partnership." Mr. Schulhof's business required frequent trips to Europe, and Mrs. Schulhof would join him, turning their trips into a search for art, a quest for an exceptional work, a hunt for an intriguing artist. When they went to Milan, they would visit Carlo Cardazzo's Galleria del Naviglio, where they acquired works by Lucio Fontana and Piero Manzoni. They spent each summer in the South of France. They would travel to every museum exhibition devoted to one of "their" artists. Mrs. Schulhof was one of the first American collectors to champion the work of European artists of the postwar period, a commitment she terms "adventuresome." As a result, their collection stands out among American collections for its inclusion of European postwar art, encompassing work by artists from Italy (Afro, Alberto Burri, Fontana, Manzoni), the United Kingdom (Barbara Hepworth, Henry Moore, Ben Nicholson, Bridget Riley), Spain (Eduardo Chillida, Joan Miró, Antoni Tàpies), France (Jean Dubuffet, Yves Klein, Pierre Soulages), and Belgium (Pol Bury). Of equal importance in the collection are the works by American artists: Carl Andre, Alexander Calder, Willem de Kooning, Jasper Johns, Donald Judd, Ellsworth Kelly, Sol LeWitt, Agnes Martin, Mark Rothko, Robert Ryman, and Cy Twombly, among others. Mrs. Schulhof has counted most of these artists among her friends.

Throughout the years I have enjoyed listening to Mrs. Schulhof's recollections of her personal life, the art she loves, and especially the artists she has met and whose work she has collected. The following conversation is a collage of the many conversations I have had with her from 1998 to the present.

What were the first works of art that had a profound impact on you?

I never dreamed I would one day collect art. In 1947 we moved to Kings Point, in Great Neck, Long Island. I had always been interested in art but didn't devote myself to it until there was a fundraiser at an ice-skating rink; it was an art auction, and I volunteered to help organize the art exhibit, which included the works of many young abstractionists. I saw a work by Jackson Pollock there. It was the first time I had seen his work. It stopped me dead in my tracks. I had never seen anything quite like it. It was a total departure from anything that I'd seen.

Why didn't you buy it?

I wasn't ready for such a commitment then. And when I was ready, his paintings had become too expensive.

A woman saw me at the auction. She had a collection and she sort of took an interest in me because she saw how interested I was in the art. She said, "Have you ever been to MoMA?" and she told me about an art course given by Abe Chanin.[1] This was about 1947–48. I took Abe Chanin's course at the Museum of Modern Art. He was very giving of his time and knowledge. He was always lecturing.

I wanted to work, so I volunteered at the museum and I saw how they kept their files in the painting department. The files that we have for the collection were inspired by how they kept the files at the museum.

Fig. 22
Carlo Cardazzo (right), owner of the Galleria del Naviglio, Milan, with Rudolph and Hannelore Schulhof, Venice, before 1963

When my kids were older, I had Saturday afternoons free, and I took painting courses in Great Neck. I also started visiting a gallery that was right in Great Neck. I scouted it out and then brought Mr. Schulhof there.

How did you come to collect contemporary art?

We first started to look at modern art, and it just didn't do it for me until I saw contemporary. Some friends suggested we visit Justin Thannhauser's gallery. Mr. Schulhof and I walked into the gallery on Madison Avenue, and we came in with the intention of buying a painting by [Georges] Rouault. Thannhauser was an immensely charming and elegant dealer. We looked at the painting and liked it and decided we wanted to buy it, but the price was outrageously high. Thannhauser was asking a certain amount for it, and Mr. Schulhof offered him something else, and Thannhauser said, diplomatically, "It's not that—it's exactly what I'm asking for the painting." He kind of liked us and saw that we had a real love of art, and he took enough interest in us to finally say, "Look, you're both so young. Why are you trying to buy the work of a dead artist? Why don't you start collecting contemporary art?" And that did it.

I thought that buying contemporary art was pretty daring in contrast to buying works of art that had been weathered by history. However, my first purchase was a small wood figure by Chaim Gross, a contemporary artist but not at all avant-garde. A friend of mine who was also a friend of the Grosses introduced me to him. There was another piece that I loved and wanted to buy, but we could not afford it. At the time, buying art was not a priority—later my husband's paper business became more successful and we were able to buy art—but Gross generously kept the piece for me until I was able to afford it, and this was the start of a long-term friendship.

Fig. 23
Thomas M. Messer (right), director of the Solomon R.
Guggenheim Museum, with Hannelore and Rudolph
Schulhof, Solomon R. Guggenheim Museum, New York,
late 1970s

Shortly thereafter, we purchased a painting by Afro [*Yellow Country*, 1957, p. 47]. It was very scary. Which is funny to me now, because although the painting has special meaning to me, I wouldn't consider it daring. One of the first non-objective pieces we ever bought was [Jean] Arp's *Bust of Gnome* [1949, p. 49].

That is how we got started. My husband had an office in Milan, and we used to spend time in Milan. While he was working, I would check out the galleries, including the Galleria del Naviglio. Most of the things weren't our taste, but when we came to that gallery we liked what we saw.

How did you decide on what to buy?
Well, it was a real partnership. Mr. Schulhof used to say that I was the curator and he was the treasurer. If we woke up and felt we couldn't live without a work we'd seen, and if we both agreed, then we knew we had to buy it. Fortunately, Mr. Schulhof and I had similar tastes. Even if we made separate visits to an exhibit, we always chose the same sculpture or painting. We loved art. That is why I couldn't continue to collect after Mr. Schulhof died.

When did you first meet Peggy Guggenheim?
It was during the Biennale, in the late '50s/early '60s. We used to go to Venice every year. We would stay at the Gritti Palace, which was across the canal from her home. She would sit in the back of her gondola, and they would take her down the canal.

One day we visited her art collection in her home, Palazzo Venier dei Leoni. We were outside her bedroom door, and there was a painting hanging there. We weren't sure who the artist was, and I said it was [Giuseppe] Santomaso. My husband said it was someone else, and just then the door opened and she came out and said, "You are absolutely right!" and then she invited us in and spoke with us about her upcoming book. We started to talk about other artists, and she was very warm to us.

Who were some dealers who were important to you?

Sam Kootz—I met him when he was on Fifty-seventh Street. He then moved to Madison Avenue. With Sam, you became a part of his life; even if you didn't buy something, you were still his friend. He was a very definite presence—he couldn't walk into a room without having everyone mesmerized. He was very statuesque, very tall. Southern accent, Virginia born. He called me "Toots."

Sam was very, very generous with us. We had the same taste in furniture. His two brown chairs and his pipe rack were similar to ones that we had. He and my husband both smoked pipes. They spent hours cleaning their pipes, and they would play chess. They both had a similar way of dealing with things. Our [Hans] Hofmann painting came from Sam.

We knew Adrian Maeght very well too. Maeght was very important in our life. He really liked us and helped us. We went to his gallery in Paris, and we spent a lot of time with him in the South of France. Maeght had a party every summer, and [Alexander] Calder was always there. He was very nice, and a great dancer. I loved to dance with Calder. At the time, Maeght's consuming passion was [Pablo] Picasso. We never considered getting one; he was already dead and out of our reach. Maeght had a lot of artists we became close to, like Eduardo Chillida.

How did you become involved with Documenta?

I was approached by a German museum director, who asked if I could help them out. I became sort of the American ambassador to Documenta. I liked being around the artists. You would see things you normally would not see, you felt up to date with what was being done.

I first met Christo and Jeanne-Claude when I was volunteering for the director, sometime in the summer of 1968. We had some students to help install the paintings, but their attention was soon drawn to Christo and Jeanne-Claude, who were having trouble, as I recall, getting this huge, sausage-shaped structure to float like a balloon. At the time, this gigantic column of air—the *5,600 Cubic Meter Package*—was their most ambitious project. It certainly caused a sensation in Kassel and captivated everyone, especially the students, who followed Christo around like he was the Pied Piper.

Later that year I met Christo and Jeanne-Claude again when they wrapped a tower in Spoleto, Italy, and then I truly got involved with them in the 1980s. It was right after our son Ronnie was killed, and Mr. Schulhof and I promised to take Mark, Ronnie's son, to Australia as his bar mitzvah present. The night before we left, I ran into Christo. I was feeling down and wasn't looking forward to the trip so much. But when I told Christo that I was leaving the next day for Australia, his

Fig. 24

Philip Rylands (center) with Hannelore and Rudolph Schulhof, Peggy Guggenheim Collection, Venice, 1980

Fig. 25
Afro with Hannelore Schulhof, Rome, 1965

eyes lit up and he immediately began to give me a list of places to see and people to meet, and told me, "You'll love it," and we all surely did. We even went to see the coastline that he had wrapped earlier [in 1969]. Although it was no longer a Christo artwork, to see it struck me. The memory of the work lingered and made it different and special.

Our paths continued to cross, as later we were invited to the Pont Neuf wrapping in Paris [1985], and lastly, we went to Japan and California—all in the same day!—to see *The Umbrellas* [1991].

Who are some of the artists you got to know?

We went to see [Mark] Rothko when he was in Rome in 1966. The space he was working in had large windows, open wide above the Renaissance piazza. He was listening to Italian opera music—*Don Giovanni*, I think.

Afro lived in Rome, but we first met him in Venice in 1956, at the Venice Biennale, where he received the honor of best Italian artist. He had been widowed, so he was ready to attach himself to someone. We had a great friend in him; we had a real friendship. We bought a painting of his in 1957, *Paese giallo* [*Yellow Country*]. Then he invited us to his studio in Rome. We fell in love with his paintings. It was the first abstract work I fell in love with. He also made jewelry on the side, and Mr. Schulhof liked what he did very much and got me a few things, a pin and matching earrings and dressy earrings. These earrings are like little creatures. I wear them every day. Through Afro, we went to a lot of other artists' studios. He took us to [Cy] Twombly's studio in Rome. We met Alberto Burri through Afro, too, and when we went to Rome in 1966 we visited his studio and bought *Bianco B* [*White B*, 1965, p. 55] directly from him. We also met Lucio Fontana through Afro. Afro was wonderful.

We met Joseph Cornell when Jean Leering, director of the Van Abbemuseum in Eindhoven, asked me to go with him to Cornell's house. I went, and he wouldn't let us come in; he left us in the garage. But we talked to him, and he was so completely informed about everything. When Mr. Schulhof and I went to visit him later, he would only allow me in and made Mr. Schulhof wait outside. Mr. Schulhof said, "Forget it," and we left! Afterwards he called me up and said, "You were interested in this and this; I'll let you have it." When he saw we liked something, quality wise, he got friendlier, more open. He asked me to catalogue his work.

Pol Bury we met in the South of France when he had a show with Maeght in the late 1960s. We saw his work *Forty Cylinders on a Plane* [1969], fell in love with it, and bought it. Then when he came to New York he came to see us. He brought his lady friend, and later he told us he was getting married. We had the wedding in the garden. It was the first time that Maeght went out of his place—he came to the wedding. Louise Nevelson, who also lived in Great Neck, attended the wedding.

After we saw Chillida's work in the South of France, Maeght took us to see him in Spain. We loved his work, and in 1968 we bought the oak piece [*Meeting Place*, 1964, p. 69]. We had been in Houston in 1966 when there was an exhibition of Chillida's work at the Museum of Fine Arts; we had seen that piece in the show, and, well, we didn't forget it. We only had it for a short time when we were asked to loan it to the Kunsthaus Zürich for a Chillida retrospective in 1969. I think Maeght also asked us to loan it to a show at his foundation in the South of France before or after the show in Switzerland. The work was wrapped and crated and picked up from our home and delivered to Kennedy airport for international shipping, but it never arrived in Europe. Our Chillida was stolen. A detective found out that it had never been sent. We received a ransom note; the kidnappers wanted money. We attempted to pay the ransom and tried desperately to find it, but it was futile. Mr. Schulhof informed the Art Dealers Association of America about the theft, and a notice was circulated to many dealers and the authorities, including Interpol and the FBI. There was even an illustration of it in the catalogue for the Chillida exhibition at the Staatliche Kunsthalle Baden-Baden in 1978, with the caption, "Lost. Reproduced in the hope that the piece might be found again." And still we didn't get it back—until seventeen years later, when it was found in a little gallery in Italy. This was in 1986. Mr. Schulhof got a call from Maeght, who said, "Are you sitting down? She's alive." But we didn't trust that it was true until we saw it.

Fig. 26
Eduardo Chillida's *Meeting Place* (*Lugar de encuentros*, 1964) in the Schulhofs' Kings Point residence, 2010

We reluctantly negotiated with the Italian dealer who had it, and in the end, to get our piece back, we had to buy it for a second time. The irony is the title, which I like to translate as *Until We Meet Again*…

Since that time, I have very rarely lent out work from the collection. We lent the triple flag [*Three Flags*, 1960, p. 97] to the [Jasper] Johns retrospective at MoMA in 1996, but that's pretty much it.

The first time I saw Agnes Martin's painting was at Elkon Gallery [in New York]. There is a cute story. We saw her at a reception once, and she came over to us and asked, "Do you have any of my paintings?" "Yes, ten of them." "Then you must be Mrs. Schulhof." We went to see her in that little town [Cuba, NM]. You understand her paintings when you go down there, because of the flatness.

We met Robert Indiana in 1968 at Documenta. That year, the American Pop artists dominated the show, which was very exciting. I did not care that much for Pop art, but Robert Indiana was the least Pop of all the Pop artists and I liked very much what he was doing. His balance of shape, color, and drawing I found to be closely related to the Minimalists. A few years later, in 1970, we bought three of his number paintings at the Eva Lee Gallery in Great Neck [*Petit Cardinal Number Zero, Petit Cardinal Number Three*, and *Petit Cardinal Number Five* (all 1966)]. In February of 1975 he came out to visit us, and he brought us the fourth one [*Petit Cardinal Number One* (1966)]. It was a gift from him, and I was very touched. He inscribed it for us on the back of the painting. He wrote, "For Rudi and Hanna with LOVE— Nova Casa." He wrote "LOVE" with the "L" and "O" over the "V" and "E," the letter "O" tilted on its side, exactly like it is in his *LOVE* sculpture. Then we bought the sculpture *LOVE* [1972] for the garden. I still love it.

With Richard Serra, I just liked his work, and then we thought about how we could have a site-specific work, and he came out at once and chose the site where he envisioned *Schulhof Curve* [1984] for the garden. He chose the secluded area to the left of the house, which is almost like a secret garden. Well, his work is a real experience and where he placed it, in the garden, you can really engage with the sculpture and the landscape but also with the grace of his work. It was a difficult installation. A crane had to lift it over the house. We were of course terrified that it was going to fall onto the house, but the sculpture came down right into the spot. He had a lot of underground work done before his actual work was set down.

Why live with art?

Art is almost like a religion for me. It is what I believe in. It is what gives my life a dimension beyond the material world we live in. I look for the work and the commitment of the artist, someone who speaks for me, or expresses or interprets something of our time that reaches me. The experience of spending a fair amount of time with each work adds a new dimension to my way of looking at things. I feel so privileged to know artists who have contributed works of extraordinary power and beauty to the world.

Fig. 27
Hannelore Schulhof in her Kings Point residence, 2010

Any regrets?

That we didn't get a Barnett Newman painting.

What advice would you give new collectors starting out today?

Get what you love and can afford. Buy with your eyes, not your ears.

1. A. L. Chanin (1912–1968), a painter, writer, and teacher, was an influential art lecturer and educa-tor at the Museum of Modern Art, New York. He was a protégé of Alfred Barnes, having studied at the Barnes Foundation from 1931 to 1934. A prolific writer and gifted speaker, he wrote for numerous journals, including *Art News*, *Art Digest*, *The Nation*, and *Harper's Bazaar*, and gained a wider audience by speaking about art on radio programs and, in 1951, on the first color television program.

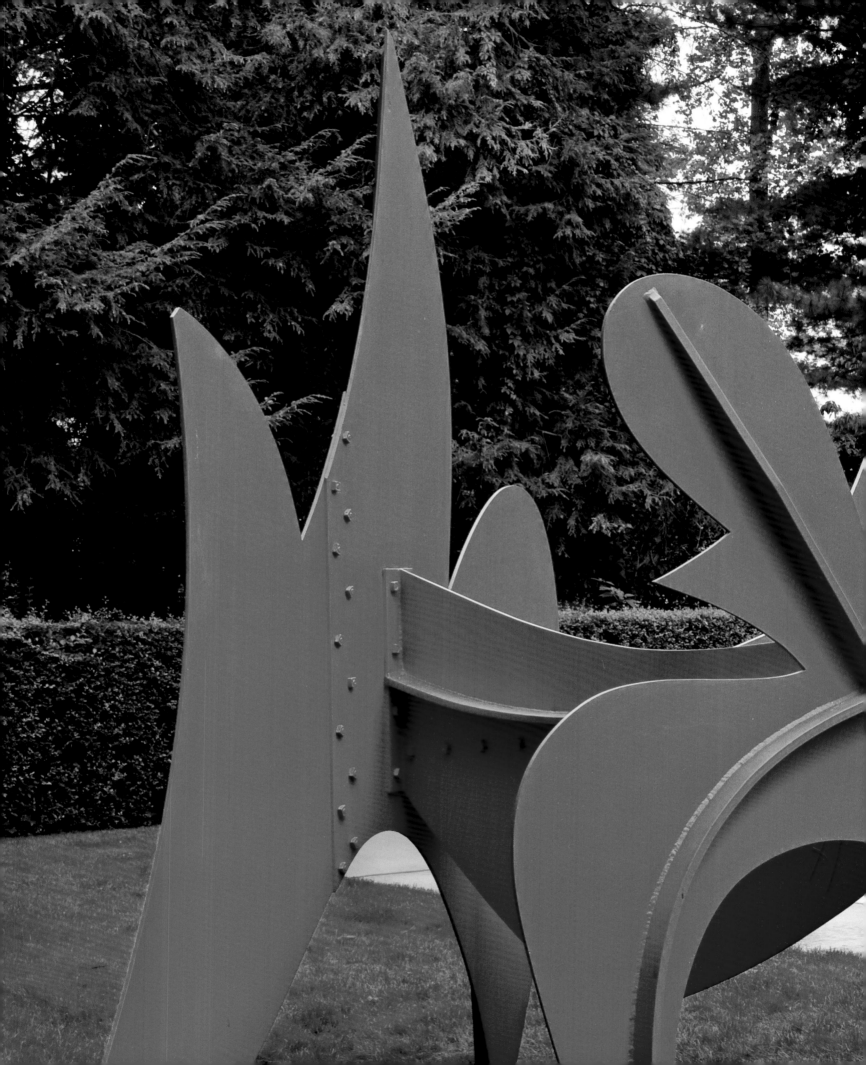

SCHULHOF COLLECTION Plates

Note

The plates illustrate a selection of works from the Hannelore B. and Rudolph B. Schulhof Collection. A listing of the promised gift of Hannelore B. Schulhof to the Solomon R. Guggenheim Foundation appears in the Catalogue of Works (pages 138–51).

Pages 44–45
Alexander Calder, *The Cow*, 1970
(detail; see pages 60–61)

AFRO
Yellow Country (Paese giallo), 1957

Oil on canvas
109.2 x 134.6 cm
Solomon R. Guggenheim Foundation, New York, Hannelore B. and Rudolph B. Schulhof Collection, promised gift of Hannelore B. Schulhof

JEAN ARP
Bust of Gnome (*Buste de Lutin*), 1949

Bronze
30.5 x 11.4 x 10.2 cm
Solomon R. Guggenheim Foundation, New York, Hannelore B. and
Rudolph B. Schulhof Collection, promised gift of Hannelore B. Schulhof

BERND and HILLA BECHER
Framework Houses, Siegen District, Germany
(Fachwerkhäuser, Siegen Sud-Westfalen), 1988

4 gelatin silver prints
Each: 104.1 x 83.8 cm
Solomon R. Guggenheim Foundation, New York, Hannelore B. and
Rudolph B. Schulhof Collection, promised gift of Hannelore B. Schulhof

JULIUS BISSIER
Still Life G (Stilleben G), July 16, 1960

Egg-oil tempera on paper
15.2 x 22.2 cm
Solomon R. Guggenheim Foundation, New York, Hannelore B. and
Rudolph B. Schulhof Collection, promised gift of Hannelore B. Schulhof

JULIUS BISSIER
Still Life K (***Stilleben K***)**, June 16, 1961**

Egg-oil tempera on paper

14 x 23.5 cm

Solomon R. Guggenheim Foundation, New York, Hannelore B. and
Rudolph B. Schulhof Collection, promised gift of Hannelore B. Schulhof

ALBERTO BURRI
White B (*Bianco B*), 1965

Oil on Masonite
151.1 x 151.1 cm
Solomon R. Guggenheim Foundation, New York, Hannelore B. and
Rudolph B. Schulhof Collection, promised gift of Hannelore B. Schulhof

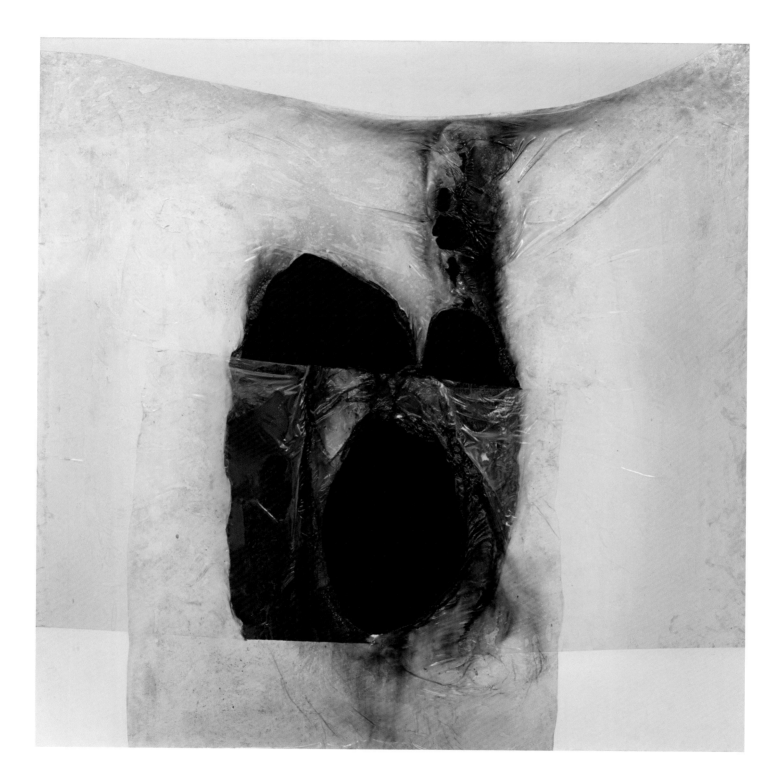

ALEXANDER CALDER
Red Disc–White Dots, 1960

Sheet metal, wire, and paint
91.4 x 88.9 x 38.1 cm
Solomon R. Guggenheim Foundation, New York, Hannelore B. and
Rudolph B. Schulhof Collection, promised gift of Hannelore B. Schulhof

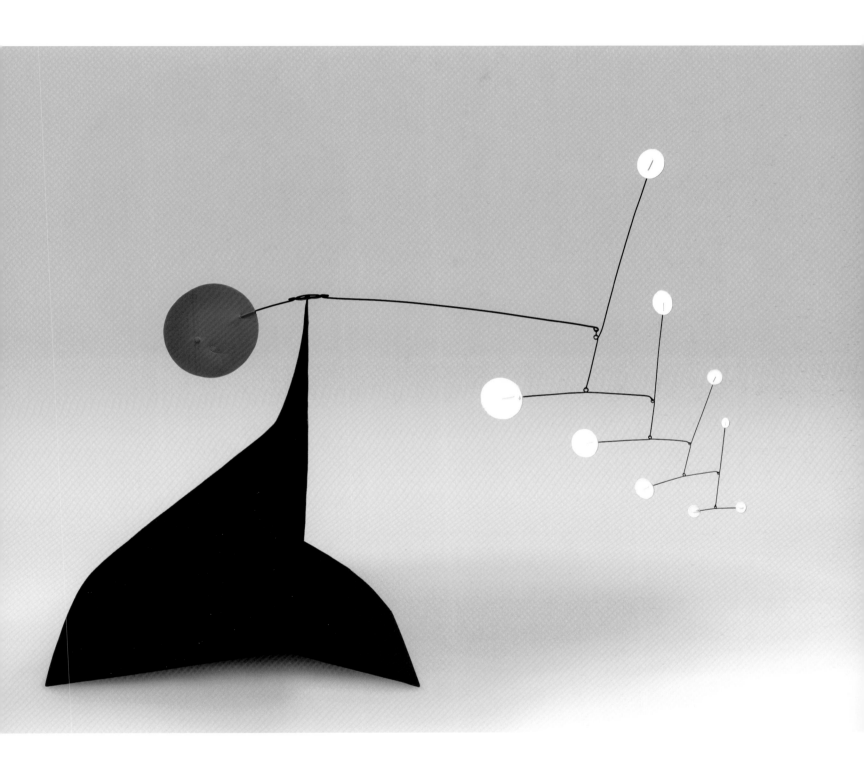

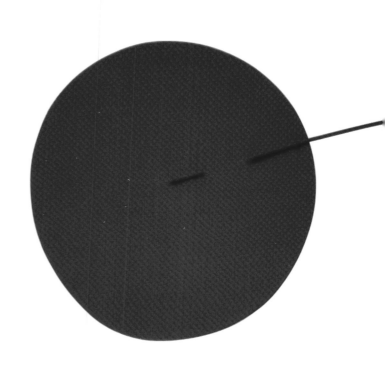

ALEXANDER CALDER
Yellow Moon, 1966

Sheet metal, wire, and paint
162.6 x 243.8 x 177.8 cm
Solomon R. Guggenheim Foundation, New York, Hannelore B. and
Rudolph B. Schulhof Collection, promised gift of Hannelore B. Schulhof

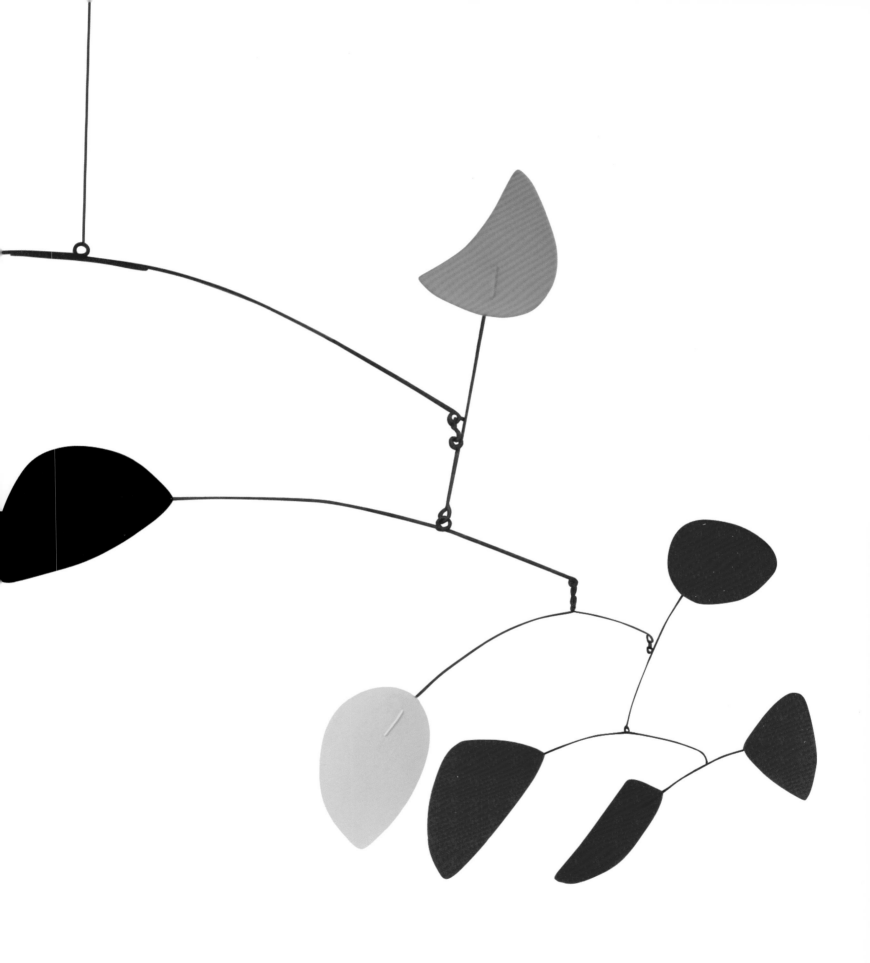

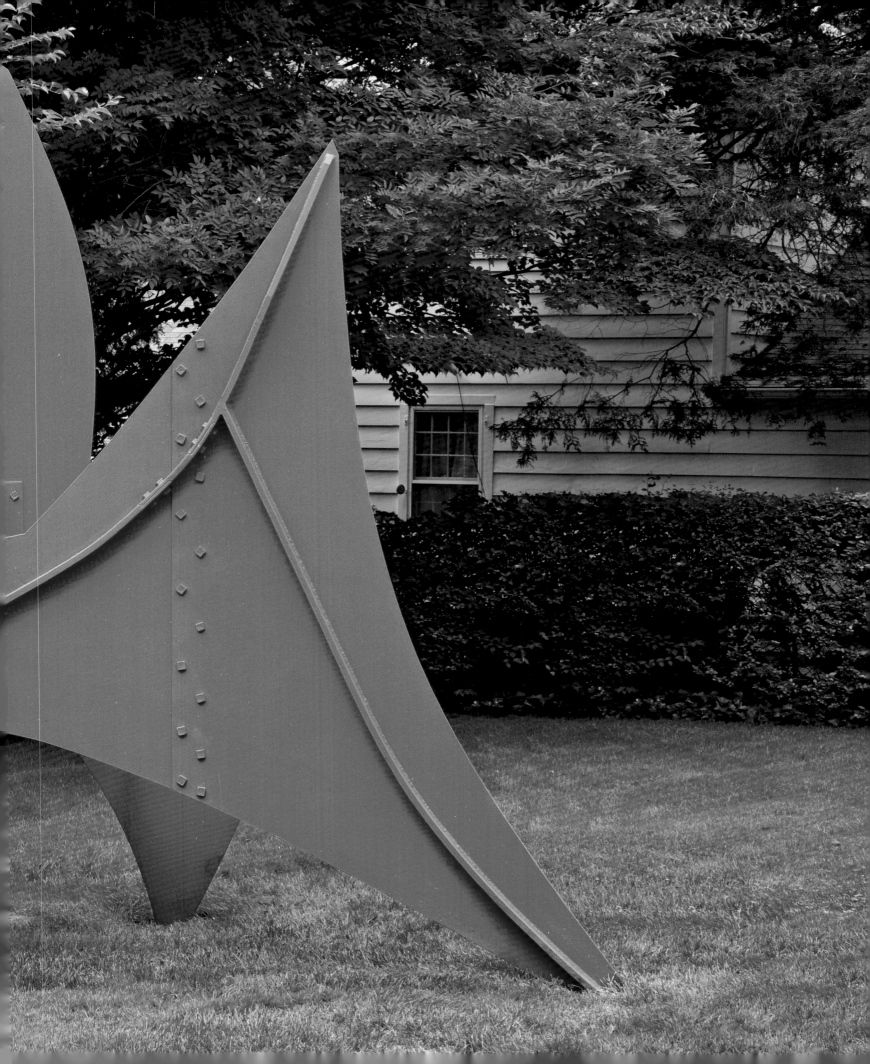

Pages 60–61

ALEXANDER CALDER
The Cow, 1970
Painted steel
304.8 x 360.7 x 248.9 cm
Solomon R. Guggenheim Foundation, New York, Hannelore B. and
Rudolph B. Schulhof Collection, promised gift of Hannelore B. Schulhof

GIUSEPPE CAPOGROSSI
Surface 236 (Superficie 236), 1957
Oil on canvas
96.5 x 71.1 cm
Solomon R. Guggenheim Foundation, New York, Hannelore B. and
Rudolph B. Schulhof Collection, promised gift of Hannelore B. Schulhof

ANTHONY CARO
Hinge, 1966

Painted steel and aluminum
101.6 x 195.6 x 254 cm
Solomon R. Guggenheim Foundation, New York, Hannelore B. and
Rudolph B. Schulhof Collection, promised gift of Hannelore B. Schulhof

EDUARDO CHILLIDA
Stele for Millares (Estela a Millares), 1960–72

Steel

174 x 160 x 125 cm

Solomon R. Guggenheim Foundation, New York, Hannelore B. and
Rudolph B. Schulhof Collection, promised gift of Hannelore B. Schulhof

EDUARDO CHILLIDA
Meeting Place (Lugar de encuentros), **1964**

Oak

78.7 x 100.3 x 100.3 cm

Solomon R. Guggenheim Foundation, New York, Hannelore B. and
Rudolph B. Schulhof Collection, promised gift of Hannelore B. Schulhof

JOSEPH CORNELL
Medici Princess, 1955

Box construction
38.1 x 25.4 x 6.4 cm
Solomon R. Guggenheim Foundation, New York, Hannelore B. and
Rudolph B. Schulhof Collection, promised gift of Hannelore B. Schulhof

TONY CRAGG
Silicate, 1988

Glass and wood
75 x 300 x 190 cm
Solomon R. Guggenheim Foundation, New York, Hannelore B. and
Rudolph B. Schulhof Collection, promised gift of Hannelore B. Schulhof

WILLEM DE KOONING
Nude Figure—Woman on the Beach, 1963

Oil on paper, mounted on canvas
81.3 x 67.3 cm
Solomon R. Guggenheim Foundation, New York, Hannelore B. and
Rudolph B. Schulhof Collection, promised gift of Hannelore B. Schulhof

MARK DI SUVERO
Untitled, 1961–62

Wood and steel
61 x 81.3 x 50.8 cm
Solomon R. Guggenheim Foundation, New York, Hannelore B. and
Rudolph B. Schulhof Collection, promised gift of Hannelore B. Schulhof

JEAN DUBUFFET
***Portrait of Soldier Lucien Geominne
(Portrait du soldat Lucien Geominne)*, 1950**

Oil on canvas
64.8 x 61.6 cm
Solomon R. Guggenheim Foundation, New York, Hannelore B. and
Rudolph B. Schulhof Collection, promised gift of Hannelore B. Schulhof

JEAN DUBUFFET
Logogriph of Blades (*Logogriphe aux pales*), 1968

Epoxy paint with polyurethene on cast polyester resin
55.2 x 57.8 x 38.1 cm
Solomon R. Guggenheim Foundation, New York, Hannelore B. and
Rudolph B. Schulhof Collection, promised gift of Hannelore B. Schulhof

JEAN DUBUFFET
Staircase VII (*Escalier VII*), 1967

Acrylic on canvas
130 x 97 cm
Solomon R. Guggenheim Foundation, New York, Hannelore B. and
Rudolph B. Schulhof Collection, promised gift of Hannelore B. Schulhof

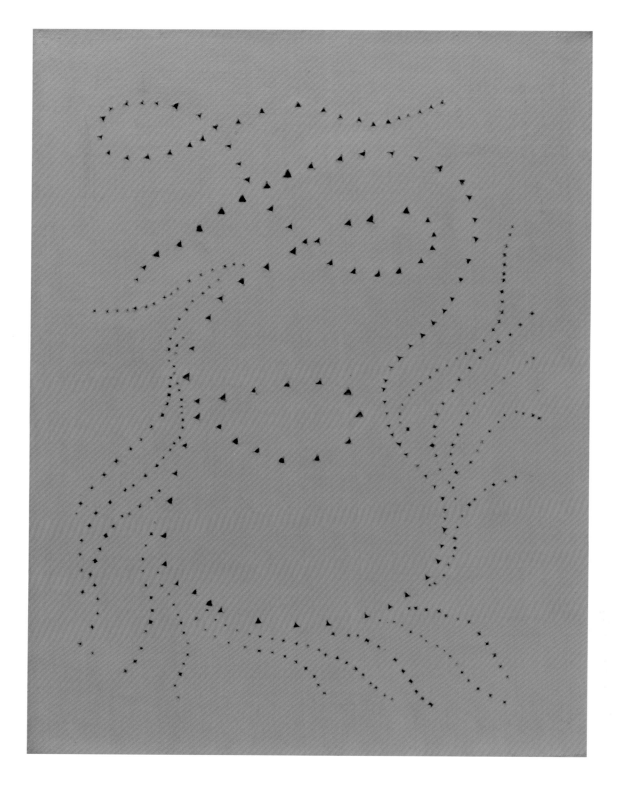

LUCIO FONTANA
Concetto spaziale, 1951

Oil on canvas
85.1 x 66 cm
Solomon R. Guggenheim Foundation, New York, Hannelore B. and
Rudolph B. Schulhof Collection, promised gift of Hannelore B. Schulhof

LUCIO FONTANA
Concetto spaziale, 1957

Oil on canvas
115.6 x 88.9 cm
Solomon R. Guggenheim Foundation, New York, Hannelore B. and
Rudolph B. Schulhof Collection, promised gift of Hannelore B. Schulhof

SAM FRANCIS
Untitled, ca. 1958

Watercolor on paper, mounted on canvas
76.2 x 56.5 cm
Solomon R. Guggenheim Foundation, New York, Hannelore B. and
Rudolph B. Schulhof Collection, promised gift of Hannelore B. Schulhof

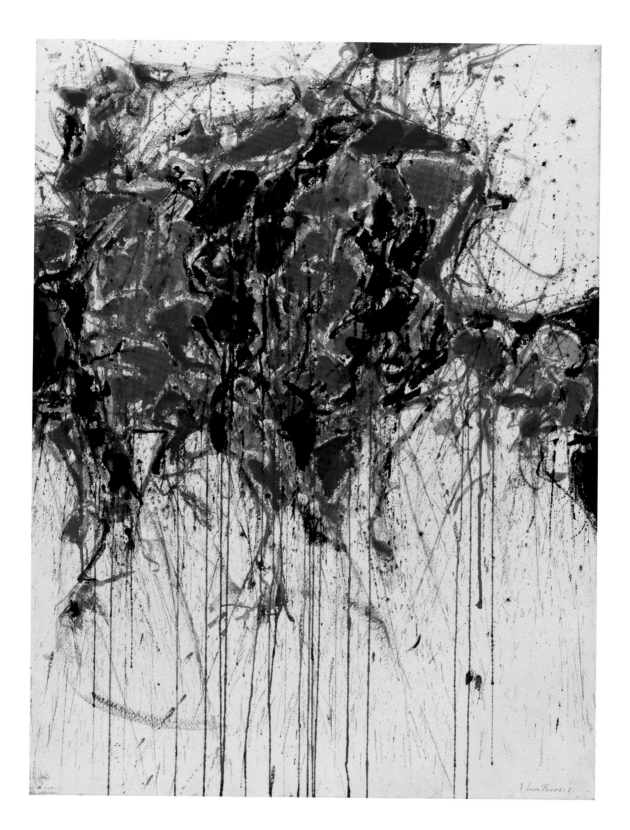

ADOLPH GOTTLIEB
Untitled, 1965

Acrylic on canvas
66 x 50.8 cm
Solomon R. Guggenheim Foundation, New York, Hannelore B. and
Rudolph B. Schulhof Collection, promised gift of Hannelore B. Schulhof

HANS HARTUNG
Composition T 1962-E15, **1962**

Oil on canvas
50.8 x 129.5 cm
Solomon R. Guggenheim Foundation, New York, Hannelore B. and
Rudolph B. Schulhof Collection, promised gift of Hannelore B. Schulhof

BARBARA HEPWORTH
Single Form (Chûn Quoit), 1961

Bronze
106 x 67.3 x 11.4 cm
Edition 3/7
Solomon R. Guggenheim Foundation, New York, Hannelore B. and
Rudolph B. Schulhof Collection, promised gift of Hannelore B. Schulhof

HANS HOFMANN
Spring on Cape Cod, 1961

Oil on canvas
121.9 x 91.4 cm
Solomon R. Guggenheim Foundation, New York, Hannelore B. and
Rudolph B. Schulhof Collection, promised gift of Hannelore B. Schulhof

JENNY HOLZER
Go Where People Sleep... **(from the** *Survival* **series), 1983–85**

Indian red granite
45.7 x 106.7 x 43.2 cm
Edition 1/2
Solomon R. Guggenheim Foundation, New York, Hannelore B. and
Rudolph B. Schulhof Collection, promised gift of Hannelore B. Schulhof

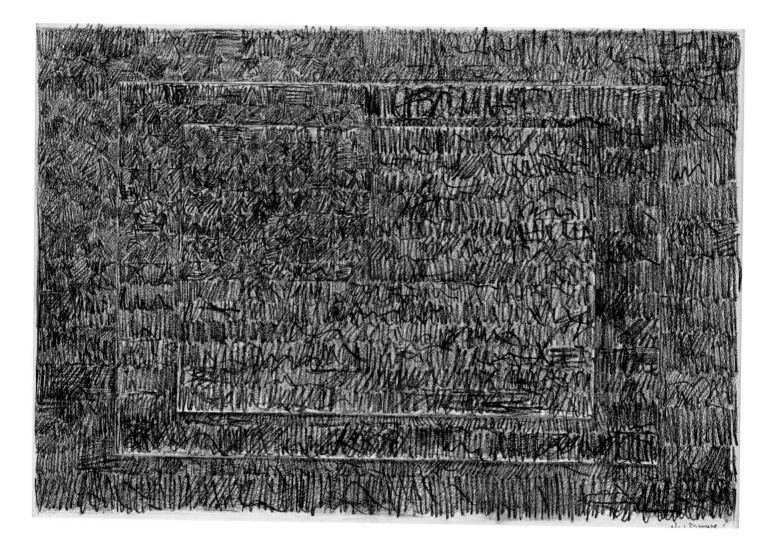

DONALD JUDD
Untitled, 1976
Clear anodized and chartreuse anodized aluminum
15.2 x 281.3 x 15.2 cm
Solomon R. Guggenheim Foundation, New York, Hannelore B. and
Rudolph B. Schulhof Collection, promised gift of Hannelore B. Schulhof

ELLSWORTH KELLY
42nd Street, 1958

Oil on canvas
151.1 x 203.2 cm
Solomon R. Guggenheim Foundation, New York, Hannelore B. and
Rudolph B. Schulhof Collection, promised gift of Hannelore B. Schulhof

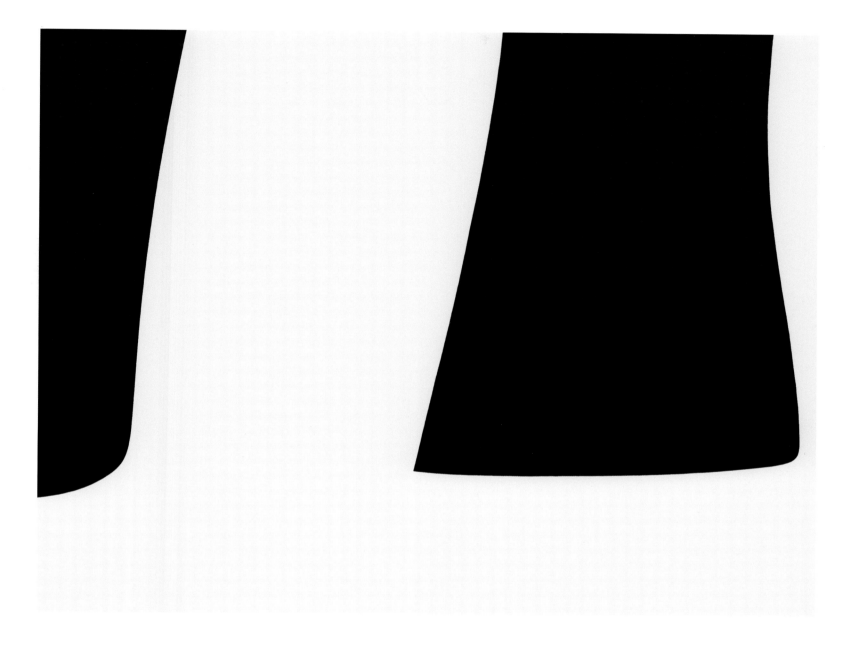

ELLSWORTH KELLY
Blue-Red, 1964

Oil on canvas
91.4 x 91.4 cm
Solomon R. Guggenheim Foundation, New York, Hannelore B. and
Rudolph B. Schulhof Collection, promised gift of Hannelore B. Schulhof

ELLSWORTH KELLY
Curve XXV, 1981

Aluminum
309.9 x 25.7 x 1.3cm
Solomon R. Guggenheim Foundation, New York, Hannelore B. and
Rudolph B. Schulhof Collection, promised gift of Hannelore B. Schulhof

ANSELM KIEFER
Your Golden Hair, Margarete (Dein goldenes Haar, Margarethe), 1981

Oil and straw on canvas
118 x 145 cm
Solomon R. Guggenheim Foundation, New York, Hannelore B. and
Rudolph B. Schulhof Collection, promised gift of Hannelore B. Schulhof

MORRIS LOUIS
#48, **1962**

Oil on canvas
203.2 x 30.5 cm
Solomon R. Guggenheim Foundation, New York, Hannelore B. and
Rudolph B. Schulhof Collection, promised gift of Hannelore B. Schulhof

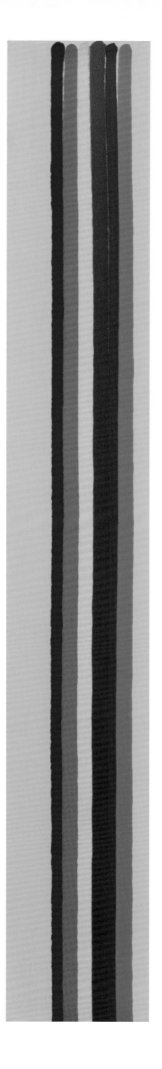

ROBERT MANGOLD
4 Color Frame Painting #9, 1984

Acrylic and pencil on paper
111.8 x 78.7 cm
Solomon R. Guggenheim Foundation, New York, Hannelore B. and
Rudolph B. Schulhof Collection, promised gift of Hannelore B. Schulhof

AGNES MARTIN
Rose, 1966

Acrylic on canvas
182.9 x 182.9 cm
Solomon R. Guggenheim Foundation, New York, Hannelore B. and
Rudolph B. Schulhof Collection, promised gift of Hannelore B. Schulhof

JOAN MITCHELL
Composition, **1962**

Oil on canvas
146.1 x 114.3 cm
Solomon R. Guggenheim Foundation, New York, Hannelore B. and
Rudolph B. Schulhof Collection, promised gift of Hannelore B. Schulhof

KENNETH NOLAND
Birth, 1961

Oil on canvas
91.4 x 91.4 cm
Solomon R. Guggenheim Foundation, New York, Hannelore B. and
Rudolph B. Schulhof Collection, promised gift of Hannelore B. Schulhof

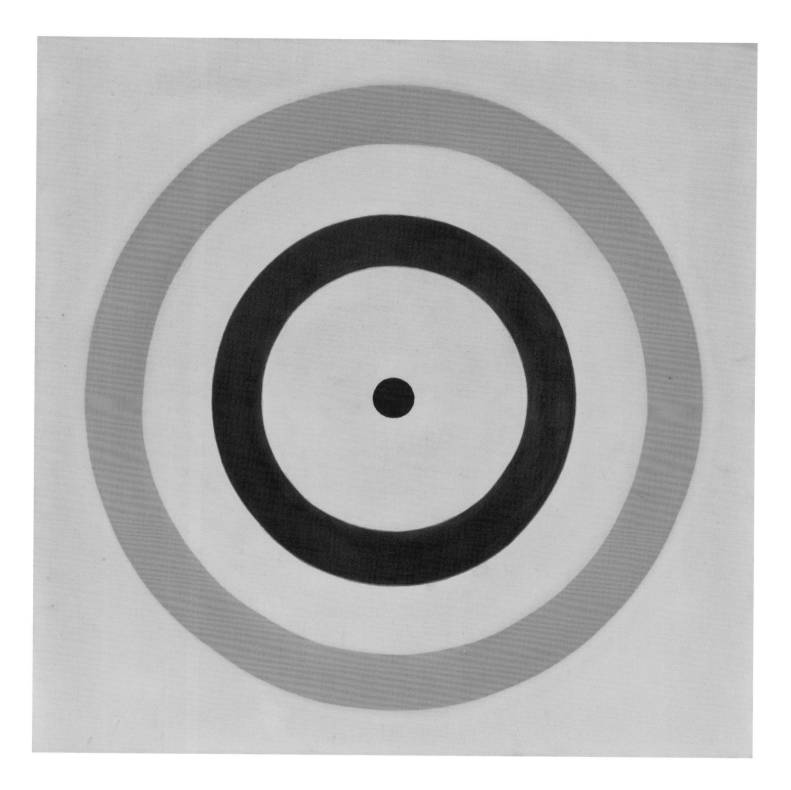

MARK ROTHKO
Red, 1968

Oil on paper, mounted on canvas
83.8 x 65.4 cm
Solomon R. Guggenheim Foundation, New York, Hannelore B. and
Rudolph B. Schulhof Collection, promised gift of Hannelore B. Schulhof

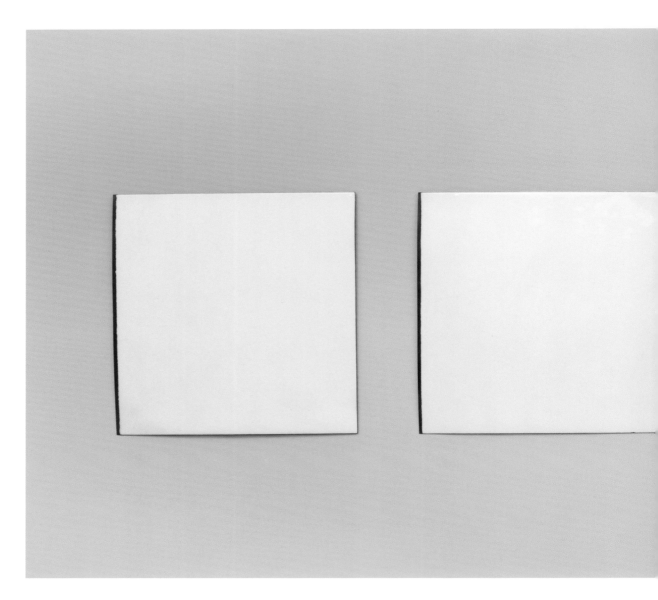

ROBERT RYMAN
Untitled, 1973

Double-baked enamel on raw copper
5 panels, each: 40.6 x 40.6 cm
Solomon R. Guggenheim Foundation, New York, Hannelore B. and
Rudolph B. Schulhof Collection, promised gift of Hannelore B. Schulhof

JOEL SHAPIRO
Untitled, 1993

Oil on wood
65.4 x 53.3 x 50.8 cm
Solomon R. Guggenheim Foundation, New York, Hannelore B. and
Rudolph B. Schulhof Collection, promised gift of Hannelore B. Schulhof

FRANK STELLA
Gray Scramble, 1968–69

Oil on canvas
175.3 x 175.3 cm
Solomon R. Guggenheim Foundation, New York, Hannelore B. and
Rudolph B. Schulhof Collection, promised gift of Hannelore B. Schulhof

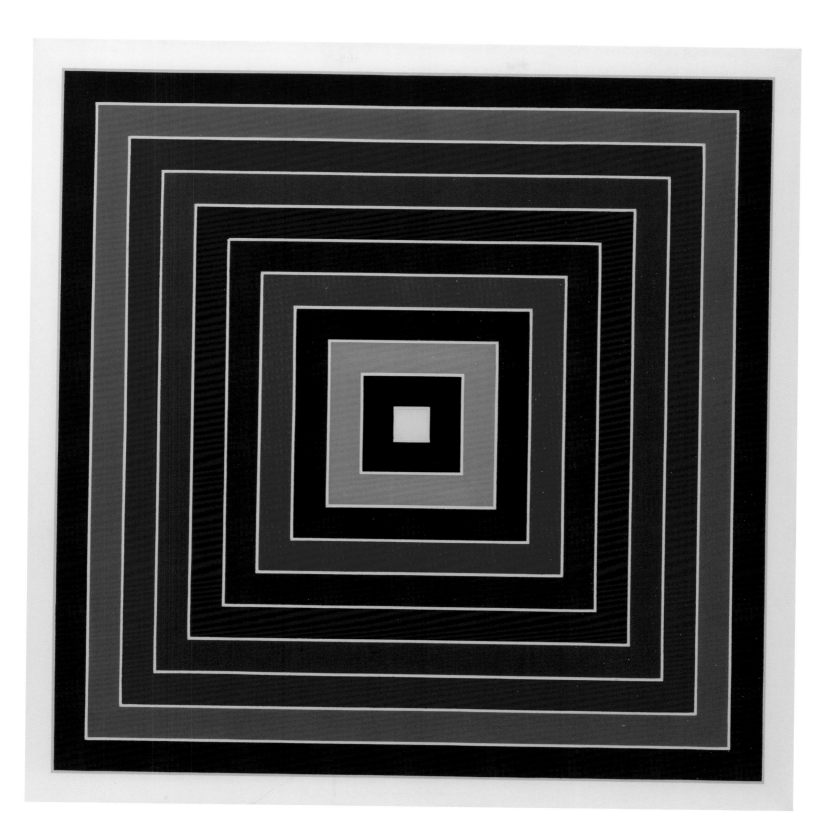

ANTONI TÀPIES
Rag and String (Chiffon et ficelle), 1967

Oil and sand on cardboard, mounted on canvas
106.7 x 74.9 cm
Solomon R. Guggenheim Foundation, New York, Hannelore B. and
Rudolph B. Schulhof Collection, promised gift of Hannelore B. Schulhof

MARK TOBEY
Trembling Space, 1961

Tempera on paper
68.6 x 50.8 cm
Solomon R. Guggenheim Foundation, New York, Hannelore B. and
Rudolph B. Schulhof Collection, promised gift of Hannelore B. Schulhof

CY TWOMBLY
Untitled, 1961

Oil and crayon on canvas

133.4 x 151.1 cm

Solomon R. Guggenheim Foundation, New York, Hannelore B. and
Rudolph B. Schulhof Collection, promised gift of Hannelore B. Schulhof

CY TWOMBLY
Untitled, 1967

Oil and crayon on canvas
127 x 170.2 cm
Solomon R. Guggenheim Foundation, New York, Hannelore B. and
Rudolph B. Schulhof Collection, promised gift of Hannelore B. Schulhof

SCHULHOF COLLECTION Documentation

Catalogue of Works

Note

This is a listing of the promised gift of Hannelore B. Schulhof
to the Solomon R. Guggenheim Foundation. Works illustrated
in the plates section are followed by the page number on which
they appear.

Pages 136–37
Hannelore and Rudolph Schulhof in their Kings Point residence, 1969

AFRO (Afro Basaldella)
(1912–1976)

***Yellow Country (Paese giallo)*,
1957**
Oil on canvas
109.2 x 134.6 cm
Solomon R. Guggenheim
Foundation, New York,
Hannelore B. and Rudolph B.
Schulhof Collection, promised
gift of Hannelore B. Schulhof

Acquired from the artist, Rome,
June 1957
p. 47

***Untitled*, 1964**
Ink on paper
17.8 x 29.8 cm
Solomon R. Guggenheim Foundation,
New York, Hannelore B. and Rudolph B.
Schulhof Collection, promised gift of
Hannelore B. Schulhof

Acquired from the artist, Rome, 1964
Inscribed "A Hannelore"

CARL ANDRE (b. 1935)

***The Way West*, 1975**
Western red cedar
2 units; each: 30.5 x 30.5 x 91.4 cm;
overall: 91.4 x 91.4 x 61 cm
Solomon R. Guggenheim Foundation,
New York, Hannelore B. and Rudolph B.
Schulhof Collection, promised gift of
Hannelore B. Schulhof

Acquired from Paula Cooper Gallery,
New York, November 1988

JEAN ARP (1886–1966)

***Bust of Gnome (Buste de Lutin)*,
1949**
Bronze
30.5 x 11.4 x 10.2 cm
Solomon R. Guggenheim Foundation,
New York, Hannelore B. and Rudolph B.
Schulhof Collection, promised gift of
Hannelore B. Schulhof

Acquired from Galleria del Naviglio,
Milan, 1957(?)
p. 49

BERND and HILLA BECHER
(Bernd Becher 1931–2007; Hilla Becher
b. 1934)

***Framework Houses, Siegen
District, Germany (Fachwerkhäuser, Siegen Sud-Westfalen)*,
1988**

4 gelatin silver prints
Each: 104.1 x 83.8 cm
Solomon R. Guggenheim Foundation,
New York, Hannelore B. and Rudolph B.
Schulhof Collection, promised gift of
Hannelore B. Schulhof

Acquired from Sonnabend Gallery,
New York, April 1989
pp. 50–51

JULIUS BISSIER (1893–1965)
Still Life (Stilleben), July 27, 1959
Egg-oil tempera on paper
17.1 x 22.9 cm
Solomon R. Guggenheim Foundation,
New York, Hannelore B. and Rudolph B.
Schulhof Collection, promised gift of
Hannelore B. Schulhof

Acquired from Lefebvre Gallery,
New York, November 1963

**Still Life G (Stilleben G),
July 16, 1960**
Egg-oil tempera on paper
15.2 x 22.2 cm
Solomon R. Guggenheim Foundation,
New York, Hannelore B. and Rudolph B.
Schulhof Collection, promised gift of
Hannelore B. Schulhof

Acquired from Lefebvre Gallery,
New York, November 1969
p. 52

**Still Life K (Stilleben K),
June 16, 1961**
Egg-oil tempera on paper
14 x 23.5 cm
Solomon R. Guggenheim Foundation,
New York, Hannelore B. and Rudolph B.
Schulhof Collection, promised gift of
Hannelore B. Schulhof

Acquired from Lefebvre Gallery,
New York, December 1963
p. 53

**Still Life H (Stilleben H),
August 20, 1962**
Egg-oil tempera on paper
17.1 x 22.2 cm
Solomon R. Guggenheim Foundation,
New York, Hannelore B. and Rudolph B.
Schulhof Collection, promised gift of
Hannelore B. Schulhof

Acquired from Lefebvre Gallery,
New York, February 1965

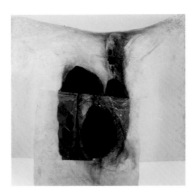

ALBERTO BURRI (1915–1995)
White B (Bianco B), 1965
Oil on Masonite
151.1 x 151.1 cm
Solomon R. Guggenheim
Foundation, New York, Hannelore B.
and Rudolph B. Schulhof Collection,
promised gift of Hannelore B.
Schulhof

Acquired from the artist, Rome, 1966
p. 55

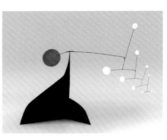

ALEXANDER CALDER
(1898–1976)
Red Disc–White Dots, 1960
Sheet metal, wire, and paint
91.4 x 88.9 x 38.1 cm
Solomon R. Guggenheim Foundation,
New York, Hannelore B. and Rudolph B.
Schulhof Collection, promised gift of
Hannelore B. Schulhof

Acquired from Pace Gallery, Boston,
October 1965
p. 57

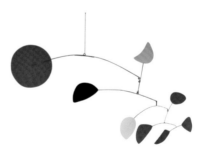

Yellow Moon, 1966
Sheet metal, wire, and paint
162.6 x 243.8 x 177.8 cm
Solomon R. Guggenheim
Foundation, New York,
Hannelore B. and Rudolph B.
Schulhof Collection, promised
gift of Hannelore B. Schulhof

Acquired from Galerie Maeght,
Paris, March 1970
pp. 58–59

The Cow, 1970
Painted steel
304.8 x 360.7 x 248.9 cm
Solomon R. Guggenheim Foundation,
New York, Hannelore B. and Rudolph B.
Schulhof Collection, promised gift of
Hannelore B. Schulhof

Acquired from Galerie
Maeght, Paris, May 1971
pp. 60–61

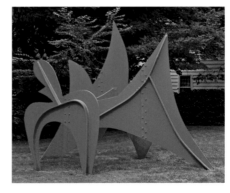

GIUSEPPE CAPOGROSSI
(1900–1972)
Surface 236 (Superficie 236), 1957
Oil on canvas
96.5 x 71.1 cm
Solomon R. Guggenheim Foundation, New York, Hannelore B. and Rudolph B. Schulhof Collection, promised gift of Hannelore B. Schulhof

Acquired from Galleria del Naviglio, Milan, October 1961
p. 63

ANTHONY CARO (b. 1924)
Hinge, 1966
Painted steel and aluminum
101.6 x 195.6 x 254 cm
Solomon R. Guggenheim Foundation, New York, Hannelore B. and Rudolph B. Schulhof Collection, promised gift of Hannelore B. Schulhof

Acquired from André Emmerich Gallery, New York, 1974
pp. 64–65

LAL, 1966
Painted steel
243.8 x 76.2 x 20.3 cm
Solomon R. Guggenheim Foundation, New York, Hannelore B. and Rudolph B. Schulhof Collection, promised gift of Hannelore B. Schulhof

Acquired from André Emmerich Gallery, New York, November 1966

JOHN CHAMBERLAIN (b. 1927)
Tiny Piece #1, 1961
Enamel paint on metal
16.5 x 25.4 x 22.9 cm
Solomon R. Guggenheim Foundation, New York, Hannelore B. and Rudolph B. Schulhof Collection, promised gift of Hannelore B. Schulhof

Acquired from Leo Castelli Gallery, New York, May 1983

EDUARDO CHILLIDA
(1924–2002)
Stele for Millares
(Estela a Millares), 1960–72
Steel
174 x 160 x 125 cm
Solomon R. Guggenheim Foundation, New York, Hannelore B. and Rudolph B. Schulhof Collection, promised gift of Hannelore B. Schulhof

Acquired from Galerie Maeght, Paris, July 1983
p. 67

Meeting Place
(Lugar de encuentros), 1964
Oak
78.7 x 100.3 x 100.3 cm
Solomon R. Guggenheim Foundation, New York, Hannelore B. and Rudolph B. Schulhof Collection, promised gift of Hannelore B. Schulhof

Acquired from Galerie Maeght, Paris, January 1968
p. 69

Untitled, 1970
Ink and collage on paper
20.3 x 27.9 cm
Solomon R. Guggenheim Foundation, New York, Hannelore B. and Rudolph B. Schulhof Collection, promised gift of Hannelore B. Schulhof

Acquired from the artist, San Sebastián, Spain, 1970
Inscribed "for Hannelore and Ruda"

Untitled, 1974
Collage on paper
55.2 x 44.8 cm
Solomon R. Guggenheim Foundation, New York, Hannelore B. and Rudolph B. Schulhof Collection, promised gift of Hannelore B. Schulhof

Acquired from Galerie Maeght, Paris, March 1975

JOSEPH CORNELL (1903–1972)
Medici Princess, **1955**
Box construction
38.1 x 25.4 x 6.4 cm
Solomon R. Guggenheim Foundation,
New York, Hannelore B. and Rudolph B.
Schulhof Collection, promised gift of
Hannelore B. Schulhof

Acquired from Galerie Daniel Varenne,
Paris, 1975
p. 71

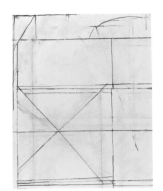

RICHARD DIEBENKORN
(1922–1993)
Untitled (Ocean Park), **1975**
Charcoal on paper
73.7 x 59.1 cm
Solomon R. Guggenheim Foundation,
New York, Hannelore B. and Rudolph B.
Schulhof Collection, promised gift of
Hannelore B. Schulhof

Acquired from Marlborough Gallery,
New York, December 1975

TONY CRAGG (b. 1949)
Bottles on a Shelf, **1981**
5 plastic bottles on painted wood
shelf
27.9 x 81.3 x 9.5 cm
Solomon R. Guggenheim
Foundation, New York,
Hannelore B. and Rudolph B.
Schulhof Collection, promised
gift of Hannelore B. Schulhof

Acquired from Marian Goodman
Gallery, New York, May 1983

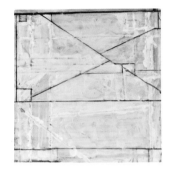

Untitled #11, **1983**
Acrylic and crayon on paper
55.9 x 53.3 cm
Solomon R. Guggenheim Foundation,
New York, Hannelore B. and Rudolph B.
Schulhof Collection, promised gift of
Hannelore B. Schulhof

Acquired from Knoedler Gallery,
New York, 1984

Silicate, **1988**
Glass and wood
75 x 300 x 190 cm
Solomon R. Guggenheim Foundation,
New York, Hannelore B. and Rudolph
B. Schulhof Collection, promised gift of
Hannelore B. Schulhof

Acquired from Marian Goodman
Gallery, New York, 1989
p. 73

MARK DI SUVERO (b. 1933)
Untitled, **1961–62**
Wood and steel
61 x 81.3 x 50.8 cm
Solomon R. Guggenheim Foundation,
New York, Hannelore B. and Rudolph B.
Schulhof Collection, promised gift of
Hannelore B. Schulhof

Acquired from John Gibson Gallery,
New York, February 1973
p. 77

WILLEM DE KOONING
(1904–1997)
Nude Figure—
Woman on the Beach, **1963**
Oil on paper, mounted on canvas
81.3 x 67.3 cm
Solomon R. Guggenheim Foundation,
New York, Hannelore B. and Rudolph B.
Schulhof Collection, promised gift
of Hannelore B. Schulhof

Acquired from Galerie Beyeler, Basel,
July 1972
p. 75

JEAN DUBUFFET (1901–1985)

Portrait of Soldier Lucien Geominne (*Portrait du soldat Lucien Geominne*), 1950
Oil on canvas
64.8 x 61.6 cm
Solomon R. Guggenheim Foundation, New York, Hannelore B. and Rudolph B. Schulhof Collection, promised gift of Hannelore B. Schulhof

Acquired from Sidney Janis Gallery, New York, April 1974
p. 79

The Cow (*La vache*), 1954
Ink on paper
32.4 x 45.7 cm
Solomon R. Guggenheim Foundation, New York, Hannelore B. and Rudolph B. Schulhof Collection, promised gift of Hannelore B. Schulhof

Acquired from Cordier & Ekstrom, New York, November 1963

The Armchair II (*Le fauteuil II*), 1966
Watercolor and ink on paper
24.8 x 16.5 cm
Solomon R. Guggenheim Foundation, New York, Hannelore B. and Rudolph B. Schulhof Collection, promised gift of Hannelore B. Schulhof

Acquired from Saidenberg Gallery, New York, May 1967

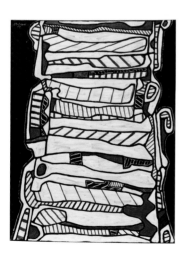

Staircase VII (*Escalier VII*), 1967
Acrylic on canvas
130 x 97 cm
Solomon R. Guggenheim Foundation, New York, Hannelore B. and Rudolph B. Schulhof Collection, promised gift of Hannelore B. Schulhof

Acquired from Pace Gallery, New York, May 1969
p. 81

Logogriph of Blades (*Logogriphe aux pales*), 1968
Epoxy paint with polyurethene on cast polyester resin
55.2 x 57.8 x 38.1 cm
Solomon R. Guggenheim Foundation, New York, Hannelore B. and Rudolph B. Schulhof Collection, promised gift of Hannelore B. Schulhof

Acquired from Pace Gallery, New York, January 1981
p. 80

Memoration XXIII (*D148*), January 5, 1979
Ink on paper with collage
50.8 x 69.9 cm
Solomon R. Guggenheim Foundation, New York, Hannelore B. and Rudolph B. Schulhof Collection, promised gift of Hannelore B. Schulhof

Acquired from Pace Gallery, New York, December 10, 1986

PERICLE FAZZINI (1913–1987)

Large Seated Woman (*Sibilla*) (*Grande donna seduta [Sibilla]*), 1947 (cast 1956)
Bronze
100.3 x 43.2 x 55.9 cm
Edition #4
Solomon R. Guggenheim Foundation, New York, Hannelore B. and Rudolph B. Schulhof Collection, promised gift of Hannelore B. Schulhof

Acquired from World House Gallery, New York, February 1963

LUCIO FONTANA (1899–1968)
Concetto spaziale, 1951
Oil on canvas
85.1 x 66 cm
Solomon R. Guggenheim Foundation,
New York, Hannelore B. and Rudolph B.
Schulhof Collection, promised gift of
Hannelore B. Schulhof

Acquired from Galleria del Naviglio,
Milan
p. 82

Concetto spaziale, 1957
Oil on canvas
115.6 x 88.9 cm
Solomon R. Guggenheim Foundation,
New York, Hannelore B. and Rudolph B.
Schulhof Collection, promised gift of
Hannelore B. Schulhof

Acquired from Galleria del Naviglio,
Milan
p. 83

SAM FRANCIS (1923–1994)
Untitled, ca. 1958
Watercolor on paper, mounted on
canvas
76.2 x 56.5 cm
Solomon R. Guggenheim Foundation,
New York, Hannelore B. and Rudolph B.
Schulhof Collection, promised gift of
Hannelore B. Schulhof

Acquired at auction, Sotheby Parke
Bernet, New York, November 5, 1985
p. 85

ADOLPH GOTTLIEB (1903–1974)
Untitled, 1965
Acrylic on canvas
66 x 50.8 cm
Solomon R. Guggenheim Foundation,
New York, Hannelore B. and Rudolph B.
Schulhof Collection, promised gift of
Hannelore B. Schulhof

Acquired from the artist, New York,
November 1967
p. 87

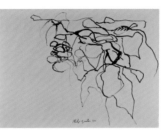

PHILIP GUSTON (1913–1980)
Still Life, 1962
Ink on paper
45.7 x 59.7 cm
Solomon R. Guggenheim Foundation,
New York, Hannelore B. and Rudolph B.
Schulhof Collection, promised gift of
Hannelore B. Schulhof

Gift of the artist, New York, 1966

Still Life, 1964
Ink on paper
45.7 x 59.7 cm
Solomon R. Guggenheim Foundation,
New York, Hannelore B. and Rudolph B.
Schulhof Collection, promised gift of
Hannelore B. Schulhof

Gift of the artist, New York, 1966

HANS HARTUNG (1904–1989)
Composition T 1962-E15, 1962
Oil on canvas
50.8 x 129.5 cm
Solomon R. Guggenheim Foundation,
New York, Hannelore B. and Rudolph B.
Schulhof Collection, promised gift of
Hannelore B. Schulhof

Acquired from the artist, Paris, 1970
pp. 88–89

BARBARA HEPWORTH
(1903–1975)
Single Form (Chûn Quoit), 1961
Bronze
106 x 67.3 x 11.4 cm
Edition 3/7
Solomon R. Guggenheim Foundation,
New York, Hannelore B. and Rudolph B.
Schulhof Collection, promised gift of
Hannelore B. Schulhof

Acquired from Gimpel Fils Gallery,
London, July 1964
p. 91

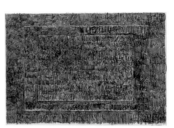

JASPER JOHNS (b. 1930)
Three Flags, 1960
Pencil on board
28.6 x 41.9 cm
Solomon R. Guggenheim Foundation,
New York, Hannelore B. and Rudolph B.
Schulhof Collection, promised gift of
Hannelore B. Schulhof

Acquired from Sonnabend Gallery,
New York, 1972
p. 97

HANS HOFMANN (1880–1966)
Spring on Cape Cod, 1961
Oil on canvas
121.9 x 91.4 cm
Solomon R. Guggenheim Foundation,
New York, Hannelore B. and Rudolph B.
Schulhof Collection, promised gift of
Hannelore B. Schulhof

Acquired from Kootz Gallery,
New York
p. 93

DONALD JUDD (1928–1994)
Untitled, 1976
Clear anodized and chartreuse anodized
aluminum
15.2 x 281.3 x 15.2 cm
Solomon R. Guggenheim Foundation,
New York, Hannelore B. and Rudolph B.
Schulhof Collection, promised gift of
Hannelore B. Schulhof

Acquired from Sonnabend Gallery,
New York, October 1978
pp. 98–99

JENNY HOLZER (b. 1950)
Go Where People Sleep...
(from the *Survival* series),
1983–85
Indian red granite
45.7 x 106.7 x 43.2 cm
Edition 1/2
Solomon R. Guggenheim Foundation,
New York, Hannelore B. and Rudolph B.
Schulhof Collection, promised gift of
Hannelore B. Schulhof

Acquired from Barbara Gladstone
Gallery, New York, January 1990
p. 95

ANISH KAPOOR (b. 1954)
Untitled, 1993
Sandstone
91.4 x 109.2 x 144.8 cm
Solomon R. Guggenheim Foundation,
New York, Hannelore B. and Rudolph B.
Schulhof Collection, promised gift of
Hannelore B. Schulhof

Acquired from Barbara Gladstone
Gallery, New York, 1994

Black Curve IV, 1972
Oil on canvas
87.9 x 104.5 cm
Solomon R. Guggenheim
Foundation, New York,
Hannelore B. and Rudolph B.
Schulhof Collection, promised
gift of Hannelore B. Schulhof

Acquired from Margo Leavin
Gallery, Los Angeles, February
1984

ELLSWORTH KELLY (b. 1923)
42nd Street, 1958
Oil on canvas
151.1 x 203.2 cm
Solomon R. Guggenheim Foundation,
New York, Hannelore B. and Rudolph B.
Schulhof Collection, promised gift of
Hannelore B. Schulhof

Acquired from Galerie Maeght, Paris,
summer 1975
p. 101

Curve XXV, 1981
Aluminum
309.9 x 25.7 x 1.3 cm
Solomon R. Guggenheim Foundation,
New York, Hannelore B. and Rudolph B.
Schulhof Collection, promised gift of
Hannelore B. Schulhof

Acquired from BlumHelman Gallery,
New York, January 1982
p. 105

Blue-Red, 1964
Oil on canvas
91.4 x 91.4 cm
Solomon R. Guggenheim
Foundation, New York,
Hannelore B. and Rudolph B.
Schulhof Collection, promised
gift of Hannelore B. Schulhof

Acquired from Galerie Maeght,
Paris, April 1970
p. 103

Green-Red, 1964
Oil on canvas
91.4 x 91.4 cm
Solomon R. Guggenheim
Foundation, New York,
Hannelore B. and Rudolph B.
Schulhof Collection, promised
gift of Hannelore B. Schulhof

Acquired from Galerie Maeght,
Paris, September 1969

ANSELM KIEFER (b. 1945)
***Your Golden Hair, Margarete
(Dein goldenes Haar,
Margarethe)*, 1981**
Oil and straw on canvas
118 x 145 cm
Solomon R. Guggenheim
Foundation, New York,
Hannelore B. and Rudolph B.
Schulhof Collection, promised
gift of Hannelore B. Schulhof

Acquired from Sonnabend
Gallery, New York, March 1984
p. 107

***Your Golden Hair, Margarete (Dein
goldenes Haar, Margarethe)*, 1981**
Gelatin silver print with paint and straw
58.7 x 83.8 cm
Solomon R. Guggenheim Foundation,
New York, Hannelore B. and Rudolph B.
Schulhof Collection, promised gift of
Hannelore B. Schulhof

Acquired from Sonnabend Gallery,
New York, February 1983

SOL LEWITT (1928–2007)
***Incomplete Open Cube 6/8*, 1974**
Painted aluminum
106.7 x 106.7 x 106.7 cm
Solomon R. Guggenheim Foundation,
New York, Hannelore B. and Rudolph B.
Schulhof Collection, promised gift of
Hannelore B. Schulhof

Acquired from Sperone Westwater
Fischer, New York, March 1977

FRANZ KLINE (1910–1962)
***Untitled*, 1951**
Ink on paper
16.5 x 21 cm
Solomon R. Guggenheim Foundation,
New York, Hannelore B. and Rudolph B.
Schulhof Collection, promised gift of
Hannelore B. Schulhof

Acquired from Marlborough-Gerson
Gallery, New York, March 1967

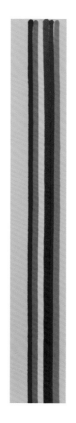

MORRIS LOUIS (1912–1962)
***#48*, 1962**
Oil on canvas
203.2 x 30.5 cm
Solomon R. Guggenheim Foundation,
New York, Hannelore B. and Rudolph B.
Schulhof Collection, promised gift of
Hannelore B. Schulhof

Acquired from Lawrence Rubin Gallery,
New York, July 1971
p. 109

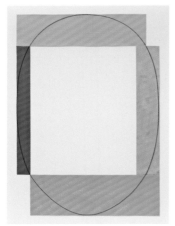

ROBERT MANGOLD (b. 1937)
4 Color Frame Painting #9, 1984
Acrylic and pencil on paper
111.8 x 78.7 cm
Solomon R. Guggenheim Foundation,
New York, Hannelore B. and Rudolph B.
Schulhof Collection, promised gift of
Hannelore B. Schulhof

Acquired from Paula Cooper Gallery,
New York, November 2, 1985
p. 111

BRICE MARDEN (b. 1938)
Study #5, 1976
Ink on paper
15.9 x 15.9 cm
Solomon R. Guggenheim Foundation,
New York, Hannelore B. and Rudolph B.
Schulhof Collection, promised gift of
Hannelore B. Schulhof

Acquired from Pace Gallery, New York,
1989
p. 113

MARINO MARINI (1901–1980)
Gertrude, 1952
Bronze
40.3 x 33.3 x 18.1 cm
Edition 6/6
Solomon R. Guggenheim Foundation,
New York, Hannelore B. and Rudolph B.
Schulhof Collection, promised gift of
Hannelore B. Schulhof

Acquired from Pierre Matisse Gallery,
New York

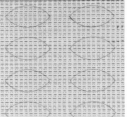

AGNES MARTIN (1912–2004)
Untitled #16, ca. 1960
Ink on paper
21.6 x 21.6 cm
Solomon R. Guggenheim Foundation,
New York, Hannelore B. and Rudolph B.
Schulhof Collection, promised gift of
Hannelore B. Schulhof

Acquired from Elkon Gallery,
New York, January 1975

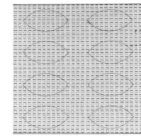

Untitled #31, 1960
Ink and pencil on paper
22.9 x 22.9 cm
Solomon R. Guggenheim Foundation,
New York, Hannelore B. and Rudolph B.
Schulhof Collection, promised gift of
Hannelore B. Schulhof

Acquired from Elkon Gallery,
New York, May 1975

Rose, 1966
Acrylic on canvas
182.9 x 182.9 cm
Solomon R. Guggenheim Foundation,
New York, Hannelore B. and Rudolph B.
Schulhof Collection, promised gift of
Hannelore B. Schulhof

Acquired from Elkon Gallery,
New York, June 1976
p. 115

JOAN MITCHELL
(1925–1992)
Composition, 1962
Oil on canvas
146.1 x 114.3 cm
Solomon R. Guggenheim
Foundation, New York,
Hannelore B. and Rudolph B.
Schulhof Collection, promised gift
of Hannelore B. Schulhof

Acquired at auction, Sotheby Parke
Bernet, New York, October 20,
1977
p. 117

BARNETT NEWMAN
(1905–1970)
Untitled Etching (No. 2), 1969
Etching and aquatint on paper
79.2 x 57.5 cm
Edition 18/27
Solomon R. Guggenheim Foundation,
New York, Hannelore B. and Rudolph B.
Schulhof Collection, promised gift of
Hannelore B. Schulhof

Acquired from Knoedler Gallery,
New York, June 1969

ISAMU NOGUCHI (1904–1988)
Two Is One, 1964
Granite
26.7 x 41.9 x 61 cm
Solomon R. Guggenheim Foundation,
New York, Hannelore B. and Rudolph B.
Schulhof Collection, promised gift of
Hannelore B. Schulhof

Acquired from Cordier & Ekstrom,
New York, April 1965

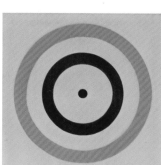

KENNETH NOLAND (1924–2010)
Birth, 1961
Oil on canvas
91.4 x 91.4 cm
Solomon R. Guggenheim Foundation,
New York, Hannelore B. and Rudolph B.
Schulhof Collection, promised gift of
Hannelore B. Schulhof

Acquired at auction, Christie's,
Manson & Woods International,
New York, May 13, 1981
p. 119

CLAES OLDENBURG (b. 1929)
*Study for a Heroic Monument in
the Form of a Bent Typewriter
Eraser*, 1970
Pencil and graphite on paper
36.8 x 29.2 cm
Solomon R. Guggenheim Foundation,
New York, Hannelore B. and Rudolph B.
Schulhof Collection, promised gift of
Hannelore B. Schulhof

Acquired from Sidney Janis Gallery,
New York, December 1970

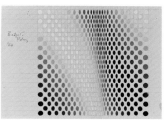

BRIDGET RILEY (b. 1931)
Black on White, 1964
Watercolor and pencil on paper
22.2 x 31.8 cm
Solomon R. Guggenheim Foundation,
New York, Hannelore B. and Rudolph B.
Schulhof Collection, promised gift of
Hannelore B. Schulhof

Acquired from Richard Feigen Gallery,
New York, December 1967

MARK ROTHKO (1903–1970)
***Red*, 1968**
Oil on paper, mounted on canvas
83.8 x 65.4 cm
Solomon R. Guggenheim Foundation,
New York, Hannelore B. and Rudolph B.
Schulhof Collection, promised gift of
Hannelore B. Schulhof

Acquired from Galleria Marlborough,
Rome, August 1968
p. 121

FRANK STELLA (b. 1936)
***Gray Scramble*, 1968–69**
Oil on canvas
175.3 x 175.3 cm
Solomon R. Guggenheim Foundation,
New York, Hannelore B. and Rudolph B.
Schulhof Collection, promised gift of
Hannelore B. Schulhof

Acquired from Lawrence Rubin Gallery,
New York, January 1971
p. 127

ROBERT RYMAN (b. 1930)
***Untitled*, 1973**
Double-baked enamel on raw copper
5 panels, each: 40.6 x 40.6 cm
Solomon R. Guggenheim Foundation,
New York, Hannelore B. and Rudolph B.
Schulhof Collection, promised gift of
Hannelore B. Schulhof

Acquired from Sperone Westwater
Fischer, New York, February 1976
pp. 122–23

ANTONI TÀPIES (b. 1923)
***Rag and String* (*Chiffon et ficelle*),
1967**
Oil and sand on cardboard, mounted
on canvas
106.7 x 74.9 cm
Solomon R. Guggenheim Foundation,
New York, Hannelore B. and Rudolph B.
Schulhof Collection, promised gift of
Hannelore B. Schulhof

Acquired from Galerie Maeght, Paris,
October 1968
p. 129

JOEL SHAPIRO (b. 1941)
***Untitled*, 1993**
Oil on wood
65.4 x 53.3 x 50.8 cm
Solomon R. Guggenheim Foundation,
New York, Hannelore B. and Rudolph B.
Schulhof Collection, promised gift of
Hannelore B. Schulhof

Acquired from PaceWildenstein,
New York, May 1995
p. 125

MARK TOBEY (1890–1976)
***Trembling Space*, 1961**
Tempera on paper
68.6 x 50.8 cm
Solomon R. Guggenheim Foundation,
New York, Hannelore B. and Rudolph B.
Schulhof Collection, promised gift of
Hannelore B. Schulhof

Acquired from Willard Gallery,
New York, November 1965
p. 131

CY TWOMBLY (b. 1928)
Untitled, 1955
Pencil on paper
55.9 x 76.2 cm
Solomon R. Guggenheim Foundation,
New York, Hannelore B. and Rudolph B.
Schulhof Collection, promised gift of
Hannelore B. Schulhof

Acquired from Hirschl & Adler Gallery,
New York, November 1984

ANDY WARHOL (1928–1987)
Flowers, 1964
Oil on canvas
61 x 61 cm
Solomon R. Guggenheim Foundation,
New York, Hannelore B. and Rudolph B.
Schulhof Collection, promised gift of
Hannelore B. Schulhof

Acquired from Galerie Denise René/
Hans Mayer, Düsseldorf, 1976

Untitled, 1961
Oil and crayon on canvas
133.4 x 151.1 cm
Solomon R. Guggenheim Foundation,
New York, Hannelore B. and Rudolph B.
Schulhof Collection, promised gift of
Hannelore B. Schulhof

Acquired at auction, Christie's, Manson
& Woods International, New York,
November 9, 1979
p. 133

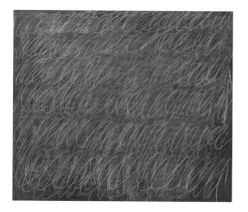

Untitled, 1967
Oil and crayon on canvas
127 x 170.2 cm
Solomon R. Guggenheim Foundation,
New York, Hannelore B. and Rudolph B.
Schulhof Collection, promised gift of
Hannelore B. Schulhof

Acquired from Leo Castelli Gallery,
New York, April 1972
p. 135

Artists' Biographies

AFRO

Afro was born Oreste Basaldella in Udine, Italy, in 1912. He trained in Florence and Venice, receiving his diploma in painting in 1931. The following year he spent some time in Milan, where, with his brother Mirko, he frequented Arturo Martini's studio. There he met Renato Birolli and Ennio Morlotti, with whom he showed at the Galleria del Milione. (The same gallery would host Afro's first solo exhibition in 1953.) In 1935 he exhibited works inspired by Corrado Cagli and the Scuola Romana at the Quadriennale of Rome.

In 1936 the decorations Afro had made for the Collegio dell'Opera Nazionale Ballila in Udine were removed due to claims that they insufficiently glorified the country's Fascist regime. The following year Afro held a solo exhibition at the Galleria della Cometa in Rome and afterward traveled to Paris, where he was profoundly inspired by the work of the Impressionists. In 1938 Afro participated in the Venice Biennale, and during World War II he taught mosaics at that city's Accademia di Belle Arti. During this period Afro also made the cartoon for the mosaics at the Palazzo dell'EUR in Rome, in which the still lifes and portraits were clearly influenced by Cubism; this was the first stage in his shift toward abstraction.

In 1950 Afro traveled to New York for a solo exhibition at the Catherine Viviano Gallery. His subsequent paintings show the influence of Arshile Gorky and the Action painting of Jackson Pollock. In 1952 he joined the Gruppo degli Otto, with whom he exhibited in 1956 at the Venice Biennale, winning the prize for best Italian painter. In 1958 he painted a large-scale mural for the UNESCO headquarters in Paris. Two years later he received the Guggenheim International Award in New York, and in 1971 the Premio Presidente della Repubblica from the Accademia di San Luca in Rome. He taught painting at the Accademia di Belle Arti in Florence until 1973 and then moved to Zurich, where he died in 1976.

CARL ANDRE

Carl Andre was born in 1935 in Quincy, Massachusetts. From 1951 to 1953 he attended the Phillips Academy in Andover, where he studied art under Patrick Morgan. After a brief enrollment in Kenyon College in Gambier, Ohio, Andre earned enough money working at Boston Gear Works to travel to England and France in 1954. The following year he joined U.S. Army Intelligence in North Carolina. In 1957 he settled in New York and worked as an editorial assistant for a publishing house. Shortly thereafter he began executing wood sculptures influenced by Constantin Brancusi and by the black paintings of his friend Frank Stella.

Andre was a leading member of the Minimalist movement, which coalesced during the early to mid-1960s. In addition to making sculpture, he began to write poems in the tradition of Concrete poetry, displaying the words on the page as if they were drawings. From 1960 to 1964 he was a freight brakeman and conductor for the Pennsylvania Railroad in New Jersey. Andre's first solo show was held in 1965 at the Tibor de Nagy Gallery in New York. In the 1970s the artist prepared numerous large-scale installations, such as *Blocks and Stones* in 1973 for the Portland Center for the Visual Arts in Portland, Oregon, and outdoor works, such as *Stone Field Sculpture* in 1977 in Hartford, Connecticut.

Notable among the many retrospectives of Andre's work are those held at the Solomon R. Guggenheim Museum, New York, in 1970; Laguna Gloria Art Museum, Austin, Texas, in 1978; Stedelijk Van Abbemuseum, Eindhoven, in 1987; Museum of Modern Art, Oxford, in 1996; Musée Cantini, Marseilles, in 1997; Open Air Museum Middelheim, Antwerp, in 2001; and Kunsthalle Basel in 2005. Andre lives and works in New York.

JEAN ARP

Jean (Hans) Arp was born in 1886 in Strasbourg. In 1904, after leaving the École des Arts et Métiers in Strasbourg, he visited Paris and published his poetry for the first time. From 1905 to 1907 Arp studied at the Akademie der Schönen Künste in Weimar, and in 1908 he attended the Académie Julian in Paris. In 1909 he moved to Switzerland and in 1911 was a founder of the Moderner Bund group there. The following year he met Robert and Sonia Delaunay in Paris and Vasily Kandinsky in Munich. Arp participated in the *Erste deutsche Herbstsalon* at the Galerie Der Sturm in Berlin in 1913. After returning to Paris the following year, he became acquainted with Guillaume Apollinaire, Max Jacob, Amedeo Modigliani, and Pablo Picasso. In 1915 he moved to Zurich, where he executed collages and tapestries, often in collaboration with his future wife Sophie Taeuber.

In 1916 Hugo Ball opened the Cabaret Voltaire, which was to become the center of Dada activities in Zurich for a group that included Arp, Marcel Janco, Tristan Tzara, and others. Arp continued his involvement with Dada after moving to Cologne in 1919. In 1922 he participated in the *Kongress der Konstruktivisten* in Weimar. Soon thereafter he began contributing to magazines such as *Merz*, *Mécano*, and *De Stijl*, and later to *La révolution surréaliste*. Arp's work appeared in the first exhibition of the Surrealist group at the Galerie Pierre in Paris in 1925, and the following year he settled in Meudon, France.

In 1931 Arp was associated with the Paris-based group Abstraction-Création and the periodical *Transition*. Throughout the 1930s and until the end of his life, he continued to write and publish poetry and essays. In 1942 he fled Meudon for Zurich, returning to Meudon after the war, in 1946. The artist visited New York in 1949 on the occasion of his solo show at Curt Valentin's Buchholz Gallery. In 1950 he was invited to execute a relief for the Harvard Graduate Center in Cambridge, Massachusetts. In 1954 Arp received the Grand Prize for Sculpture at the Venice Biennale. A retrospective of his work was held at the Museum of Modern Art in New York in 1958, followed by another at the Musée National d'Art Moderne in Paris in 1962. Arp died in 1966 in Basel.

BERND AND HILLA BECHER

Bernd Becher was born in 1931 in Siegen, Germany. He studied painting and lithography at the Staatliche Akademie der Bildenden Künste in Stuttgart from 1953 to 1956 and typography at the Staatliche Kunstakademie Düsseldorf from 1957 to 1961. Hilla Becher was born Hilla Wobeser in 1934 in Potsdam, Germany. She studied graphic and printing techniques at the Kunstakademie Düsseldorf, where she met Bernd Becher. The two artists first collaborated in 1959 and were married in 1961. They began working as freelance photographers, concentrating on industrial photography.

From their first series of photographs of water towers, the artists did not veer from architectural portraiture subjects, using both industrial and domestic structures, such as gas tanks, silos, framework houses, and the like. They were given their first gallery show in 1963 at the Galerie Ruth Nohl in Siegen, and by 1968 they were exhibiting in the United States as well as in European cities outside Germany. In 1969 the artists called the architectural subject matter of their photographs "anonymous sculpture."

In 1972 the Bechers began showing at the Sonnabend Gallery in New York. In 1974 the Institute of Contemporary Arts in London organized an exhibition of their work, which toured the United Kingdom. They were invited to participate in Documenta in Kassel in 1972, 1977, 1982, and 2002, and at the São Paulo Bienal in 1977. The Stedelijk Van Abbemuseum in Eindhoven organized a retrospective of the artists' work in 1981. In 1985 they had a major museum exhibition, which traveled to the Museum Folkwang Essen, Musée d'Art Moderne de la Ville de Paris, and Musée d'Art Moderne de la Ville de Liège, Belgium. In 1991 the artists won the Golden Lion for sculpture at the Venice Biennale. The Venice installation was reworked later in 1991 in a retrospective exhibition at the Kunstverein in Cologne, and was shown again in 1994 at the Ydessa Hendeles Art Foundation in Toronto and at the Westfälisches Landesmuseum für Kunst und Kulturgeschichte in Münster. In 2002 the Bechers were awarded the Erasmus Prize in recognition of their instrumental roles as professors at the Kunstakademie Düsseldorf. Other retrospectives of the couple's work have been organized by the Photographische Sammlung/SK Stiftung Kultur in Cologne (1999 and 2003), Centre Georges Pompidou in Paris (2005), and Museum of Modern Art in New York (2008). Bernd Becher died in 2007 in Rostock, Germany.

JULIUS BISSIER

Julius Bissier was born in 1893 in Freiburg, Germany. After briefly studying art history at the Universität Freiburg in 1913, he began attending the Kunstakademie Karlsruhe the following year but was forced into military service after just a few months. He returned to Freiburg in 1918 and began a career as a self-taught painter. In 1919 Bissier met the ethnologist and art historian Ernst Grosse, who introduced him to East Asian mysticism and art. His first exhibition was held at the Kunstverein in Freiburg in 1920.

Bissier's early paintings were strongly influenced by so-called primitive German painters, but in 1923 he began working in a realist style aligned with Der Neue Sachlichkeit. From 1929 to 1934 he taught at the Universität Freiberg, during which time his work became increasingly abstract, perhaps as a result of a visit to Constantin Brancusi in his Paris studio, as well as his friendship with Willi Baumeister, who introduced him to work by Georges Braque, Paul Klee, Fernand Léger, and Pablo Picasso, among others, in his Frankfurt studio. In 1930 he began creating works on paper using tusche applied with a brush; he would work on these drawings almost exclusively between 1932 and 1947. A fire at the Universität Freiberg in 1934 destroyed almost all of Bissier's works up to that point.

In 1939 Bissier moved to Hagnau, Germany, on Lake Constance, where he started designing carpets and fabrics, which were made by his wife, Lisbeth, a weaver. In 1942 he met the potter Richard Bampi and began experimenting with ceramics, occasionally in Bampi's workshop. The following year Bissier reintroduced color into his work. He began to produce colorful monotypes in 1947 and became interested in woodcuts and ink drawings from India. In 1955 he began a series of miniatures in tempera and watercolor.

In 1959 the Gemeentemuseum in the Hague presented a retrospective exhibition of Bissier's work. That same year, and in 1964, he participated in Documenta in Kassel, and in 1960 in the Venice Biennale. At the São Paulo Bienal the following year Bissier was awarded the Tenth Anniversary Award. Numerous international exhibitions and awards followed, including the Bundesverdienstkreuz in 1964. In 1961 he moved to Ascona, Switzerland, where he died in 1965.

ALBERTO BURRI

Alberto Burri was born in 1915 in Città di Castello, Italy. He earned a medical degree from the Università di Perugia in 1940 and served as a physician during World War II. Following his unit's capture in northern Africa, he was interned in a prisoner-of-war camp in Hereford, Texas, in 1944, where he started to paint on the burlap that was readily at hand. After his release in 1946, Burri moved to Rome, where his first solo show was held at the Galleria La Margherita the following year.

Like many Italian artists of his generation who reacted against the politicized realism popular in the late 1940s, Burri soon turned to abstraction, becoming a proponent of Art Informel. Around 1949–50 he experimented with various unorthodox materials, fabricating tactile collages with pumice, tar, and burlap. At this time he also commenced the *Mold* (*Muffa*) and *Hunchback* (*Gobbo*) series; the latter are humped canvases that break with the traditional two-dimensional plane. This preoccupation with the ambiguity of the pictorial surface and with non-art materials led Burri to help start Gruppo Origine, founded by Italian artists in 1950 in opposition to the increasingly decorative nature of abstraction. The artists in Gruppo Origine exhibited their work together in 1951 at the Galleria dell'Obelisco, Rome.

In 1953 Burri garnered attention in the United States when his work was included in the group exhibition *Younger European Painters* at the Solomon R. Guggenheim Museum in New York and was shown as well at the Frumkin Gallery in Chicago and the Stable Gallery in New York. In the mid-1950s he began burning his mediums, a technique he termed *combustione*. These charred wood and burlap works were first exhibited in 1957 at the Galleria dell'Obelisco. In 1958 his welded iron sheets were shown at the Galleria Blu in Milan. That same year Burri was awarded Third Prize at the Carnegie International in Pittsburgh. In 1959 he won the Premio dell'Ariete in Milan and the UNESCO Prize at the São Paulo Bienal. There was a solo show of Burri's art in 1960 at the Venice Biennale, where he was awarded the Critics' Prize.

Persevering with the *combustione* technique, Burri started to burn plastic in the early 1960s. These works were exhibited in 1962 at the Marlborough Galleria d'Arte in Rome. Burri's first retrospective in the United States was presented by the Museum of Fine Arts in Houston in 1963. His art was selected for the traveling *Premio Marzotto* exhibition of 1964–65, for which he won the prize in 1965, the same year in which he was awarded the Grand Prize at the São Paulo Bienal. In 1972 the Musée National d'Art Moderne in Paris dedicated a retrospective to Burri. In the early 1970s Burri embarked upon the "cracked" paintings series, featuring creviced, earthlike surfaces that play with notions of trompe l'oeil. A retrospective of Burri's work was inaugurated at the Frederick S. Wight Gallery at the University of California, Los Angeles, in 1977; it traveled to the Marion Koogler McNay Art Institute in San Antonio and the Solomon R. Guggenheim Museum in New York in 1978.

Burri turned to another industrial material, Cellotex, in 1979, and continued to use it throughout the 1980s and 1990s. In 1994 the Italian Order of Merit was bestowed upon Burri. The artist died in 1995 in Nice, France.

ALEXANDER CALDER

Alexander Calder was born in 1898 in Lawnton, Pennsylvania. In 1919 he received an engineering degree from Stevens Institute of Technology in Hoboken, New Jersey. Calder attended the Art Students League in New York from 1923 to 1926, studying briefly with Thomas Hart Benton and John Sloan. As a freelance artist for the *National Police Gazette* in 1925, he spent two weeks sketching at the circus; his fascination with the subject dated from this time. He also made his first sculpture in 1925, and the following year he made several constructions of animals and figures with wire and wood. Calder's first exhibition of paintings took place in 1926 at the Artist's Gallery in New York. Later that year he went to Paris and attended the Académie de la Grande Chaumière.

In Paris he met Stanley William Hayter, exhibited at the 1926 Salon des Indépendants, and in 1927 began giving performances of his miniature circus. The first show of his wire animals and caricature portraits was held at the Weyhe Gallery in New York in 1928. That same year he met Joan Miró, who became his lifelong friend. Subsequently Calder divided his time between France and the United States. In 1929 Galerie Billiet gave him his first solo show in Paris. He met Frederick Kiesler, Fernand Léger, and Theo van Doesburg and visited Piet Mondrian's studio in 1930. Calder began to experiment with abstract sculpture at this time and in 1931 and 1932 introduced moving parts into his work. These moving sculptures were called "mobiles"; the stationary constructions were to be named "stabiles."

Calder exhibited with the Abstraction-Création group in Paris in 1933. In 1943 the Museum of Modern Art in New York gave him a solo exhibition. During the 1950s Calder traveled widely and executed *Towers* (wall mobiles) and *Gongs* (sound mobiles). He won the Grand Prize for Sculpture at the 1952 Venice Biennale. Late in the decade, the artist worked extensively with gouache. From this period on, he executed numerous major public commissions. In 1964–65 the Solomon R. Guggenheim Museum in New York presented a Calder retrospective. He began the *Totems* in 1966 and the *Animobiles* in 1971; both are variations on the standing mobile. A Calder exhibition was held at the Whitney Museum of American Art in New York in 1976. Calder died in 1976 in New York.

GIUSEPPE CAPOGROSSI

Giuseppe Capogrossi was born in 1900 in Rome. After earning a law degree in 1922, he decided to become an artist and began to study under the fresco painter Giambattista Conti, and later at the studio of Felice Carena. Around the same time he formed a close relationship with the painter Emanuele Cavalli, an association that would last some twenty years. In 1925 he attended the Casa d'Arte Bragaglia, and between 1927 and 1933 he traveled several times to Paris, where he became particularly interested in the work of Pablo Picasso, Amedeo Modigliani, and Pierre-Auguste Renoir.

In 1928 Capogrossi was invited to show at the Venice Biennale, and in 1932 he participated in the *III Mostra del Sindacato Regionale Fascista Belle Arti del Lazio* in Rome, showing paintings that revealed the influence of his time in Paris, including *Harlequin (Arlecchino*, 1931) and *Woman with a Veil (Donna con velo*, 1931). In early 1933 Capogrossi exhibited with Corrado Cagli and Cavalli (as part of the loosely associated group known as the Scuola Romana) at the Galleria del Milione in Milan, the epicenter of Italian abstract art. The reserved, pale color palette and subtle geometric cadences of his works from this period, including *Tiber in Full Spate (Piena sul Tevere*, 1934) and *Tiber Poet (Il poeta del Tevere*, 1933), suggest his tutelage under fresco painters. Capogrossi was featured in several major exhibitions of Italian artists in the 1930s, including *Exposition des peintres romains* in Paris in 1933 and the Quadriennale of Rome in 1935; following the latter, critics recognized him as one of the major figures in the renewal of Roman painting. In 1939 he was given his own room at the Quadriennale of Rome.

The postwar years saw Capogrossi paint his first abstract works, and by the end of 1949 he had developed a distinct post-Cubist vocabulary of his own, formalizing a language of signs that involved the arrangement of comblike matrices in compositions that were at once logical and free, aligning him closely with the Art Informel movement. In 1951 he co-founded the Gruppo Origine with Mario Ballocco, Alberto Burri, and Ettore Colla, through which they hoped to promote the ideals of abstract art, including a reductive simplicity of expression. Capogrossi also worked as a teacher for a large part of his career, serving at the Liceo Artistica in Rome from 1946 to 1965 and at the Accademia di Belle Arti in Naples from 1965 to 1970. He participated in Documenta in Kassel in 1955 and 1959, and in 1974 the Galleria Nazionale d'Arte Moderna in Rome organized a major retrospective of his oeuvre. Capogrossi died in 1972 in Rome.

ANTHONY CARO

Anthony Caro was born in 1924 in New Malden, England. From 1942 to 1944 he studied at Christ's College in Cambridge, attending Farnham School of Art during his holidays and graduating with a degree in engineering. Beginning in 1946, after returning from naval service during World War II, he studied sculpture at the Regent Street Polytechnic in London and then at the Royal Academy from 1947 to 1952. From 1951 to 1953 he worked as Henry Moore's assistant and taught at St. Martin's School of Art in London. During this period he worked extensively in clay and plaster, and his sculptures were mainly figurative.

In 1956 Caro had his first solo exhibition at the Galleria del Naviglio in Milan, and the following year he had his first solo exhibition in London at the Gimpel Fils Gallery. After visiting the United States and meeting Robert Motherwell, Kenneth Noland, David Smith, and other artists, he went back to London in 1960 and made his first abstract steel sculptures, which were shown at the Whitechapel Gallery in 1963. With these works of brightly painted, prefabricated materials, Caro initiated and developed a new aesthetic in sculpture, one that would have a lasting effect on the future generation of artists. Although his preferred medium was steel, the artist experimented using bronze, wood, paper, and lead as well.

In 1963 Caro began a two-year teaching position at Bennington College in Vermont, and one year later he had his first solo exhibition in New York at the André Emmerich Gallery. Caro was the subject of several retrospective exhibitions during the 1960s, and he was invited to show at the 1966 Venice Biennale and the 1969 São Paulo Bienal. In 1970 he started making sculptures of nonpainted steel. Many museums have mounted exhibitions dedicated to his work, including the Museum of Modern Art, New York (1975), Tate Gallery, London (1991), Museum of Contemporary Art, Tokyo (1995), and National Gallery, London (1998). Caro has earned many prizes during his career, including the Japan Art Association's Praemium Imperiale, and he holds honorary degrees from Cambridge and Yale Universities. He was knighted in 1987 and has also been made an honorary member of the American Academy of Arts and Letters and of the Accademia di Brera, Milan.

JOHN CHAMBERLAIN

John Chamberlain was born in 1927 in Rochester, Indiana. He grew up in Chicago and, after serving in the U.S. Navy from 1943 to 1946, attended the Art Institute of Chicago from 1951 to 1952. At that time he began making flat welded sculptures influenced by the work of David Smith. In 1955 and 1956 Chamberlain studied and taught sculpture at Black Mountain College, near Asheville, North Carolina, where most of his friends were poets, including Robert Creeley, Robert Duncan, and Charles Olson. By 1957 he had begun to include scrap metal from cars in his work, and from 1959 on he concentrated on sculpture built entirely of crushed automobile parts welded together. Chamberlain's first major solo show was held at the Martha Jackson Gallery in New York in 1960.

Chamberlain's work was widely acclaimed in the early 1960s. His sculpture was included in *The Art of Assemblage* at the Museum of Modern Art in New York in 1961, and in the São Paulo Bienal the same

year. Beginning in 1962 Chamberlain showed frequently at the Leo Castelli Gallery in New York, and in 1964 his work was exhibited at the Venice Biennale. While he continued to make sculpture from auto parts, Chamberlain also experimented with other mediums. From 1963 to 1965 he made geometric paintings with sprayed automobile paint. In 1966, the same year he received the first of two fellowships from the John Simon Guggenheim Memorial Foundation, he began a series of sculptures of rolled, folded, and tied urethane foam. These were followed in 1970 by sculptures of melted or crushed metal and heat-crumpled Plexiglas. Chamberlain's work was presented in a retrospective at the Solomon R. Guggenheim Museum in New York in 1971.

In the early 1970s Chamberlain began once more to make large works from automobile parts. Until the mid-1970s the artist assembled these auto sculptures on the ranch of collector Stanley Marsh in Amarillo, Texas. These works were shown in the sculpture garden at the Dag Hammarskjold Plaza, New York, in 1973, and at the Contemporary Arts Museum in Houston in 1975. In 1977 Chamberlain began experimenting with photography taken with a panoramic Widelux camera. His next major retrospective was held at the Museum of Contemporary Art in Los Angeles in 1986; the museum simultaneously co-published *John Chamberlain: A Catalogue Raisonné of the Sculpture 1954–1985*, authored by Julie Sylvester. In 1993 Chamberlain received both the Skowhegan Medal for Sculpture and the Lifetime Achievement in Contemporary Sculpture Award from the International Sculpture Center. In 1997 Chamberlain was named a recipient of the National Arts Club's Gold Medal Visual Arts Award, and in 1999 he received the Distinction in Sculpture Honor from the Sculpture Center in New York. Over the past decade the artist has expanded his well-established career by undertaking a new medium: the large-format photograph. In 2007 he received the Academy of the Arts Lifetime Achievement Award for Visual Arts from Guild Hall in East Hampton, New York. The artist currently lives and works on Shelter Island, New York.

EDUARDO CHILLIDA

Eduardo Chillida was born in 1924 in San Sebastián, Spain. After studying architecture from 1943 to 1947 at the Universidad de Madrid, he began to concentrate on drawing and sculpture. He moved to Paris in 1948 and became close friends with Pablo Palazuelo, with whom he exhibited at the Salon de Mai of 1949. In 1950 Chillida lived in Villaines-sous-Bois, France, before moving the following year to Hernani, near San Sebastián, where he formed a friendship with José Cruz Iturbe.

Chillida's first solo exhibition was held at the Galería Clan in Madrid in 1954. The city of San Sebastián commissioned him to execute a monument to Alexander Fleming in 1955. In 1956 he was given the first of many solo exhibitions at Galerie Maeght in Paris. He won the Grand Prize for Sculpture at the Venice Biennale in 1958, and the same year he made his first visit to the United States, where he met James Johnson Sweeney, Mies van der Rohe, and the composer Edgar Varèse. Chillida was awarded the Kandinsky Prize in 1960. He traveled to Greece in 1963, and the following year he won the Sculpture Prize at the Carnegie International in Pittsburgh. In 1966 Chillida met the philosopher

Martin Heidegger, whose book *Die Kunst und der Raum* (*Art and Space*) he illustrated.

Retrospectives of Chillida's work were held in 1969 at museums in Basel, Zurich, and Munich. That same year he began a sculpture for the UNESCO Building in Paris, and the following year he executed a commission for the World Bank headquarters in Washington, D.C. In 1971 he was a visiting professor at the Carpenter Center for the Visual Arts at Harvard University, and later in the year traveled to Barcelona on the occasion of his solo exhibition at the Sala Gaspar. In 1979 Chillida and Willem de Kooning shared the Andrew W. Mellon Prize, which was accompanied by a major show at the Museum of Art of the Carnegie Institute in Pittsburgh. He was given a solo exhibition at the Solomon R. Guggenheim Museum in New York in 1980, and at the Venice Biennale in 1990 he had a solo show at the Ca'Pesaro. He received the Praemium Imperiale from the Japan Art Association in 1991. A museum dedicated to the artist's work, the Museo Chillida-Leku, opened in Hernani in 2000. The artist died in 2002 at his residence on Mount Igueldo in San Sebastián.

JOSEPH CORNELL

Joseph Cornell was born in 1903 in Nyack, New York. From 1917 to 1921 he attended the Phillips Academy in Andover, Massachusetts. He was an avid collector of memorabilia and, while working as a woolen-goods salesman in New York until 1931, developed his interests in ballet, literature, and opera. He lived with his mother and brother, Robert, at their home in the Flushing section of Queens. In the early 1930s Cornell met Surrealist writers and artists at the Julien Levy Gallery in New York and saw Max Ernst's collage-novel *La femme 100 têtes*.

Cornell's early constructions of found objects were first shown in the group exhibition *Surréalisme* at Levy's gallery in 1932. From 1934 to 1940 Cornell supported himself by working as a textile designer at the Traphagen studio in New York. During these years he became familiar with Marcel Duchamp's readymades and Kurt Schwitters's box constructions. Cornell was included in the 1936 exhibition *Fantastic Art, Dada, Surrealism* at the Museum of Modern Art in New York. Always interested in film and cinematic techniques, he made a number of movies, including the collage film *Rose Hobart* (1936), and wrote two film scenarios; one of these, *Monsieur Phot* (1933), was published in 1936 in Levy's book *Surrealism*.

Cornell's first two solo exhibitions took place at the Julien Levy Gallery in 1932 and 1939, and they included an array of objects, a number of them in shadow boxes. During the 1940s and 1950s he made *Aviary, Hotel, Observatory*, and *Medici* boxes, among other series, as well as boxes devoted to stage and screen personalities. In the early 1960s Cornell stopped making new boxes and began to reconstruct old ones and to work intensively in collage. Cornell retrospectives were held in 1967 at the Pasadena Art Museum in Pasadena, California, and the Solomon R. Guggenheim Museum in New York. In 1970 the Metropolitan Museum of Art in New York mounted an exhibition of his collages. Cornell died in 1972 at his home in Flushing, New York.

TONY CRAGG

Anthony (Tony) Cragg was born in 1949 in Liverpool. From 1969 to 1977 he studied at Gloucestershire College of Art in Cheltenham and the Wimbledon School of Art and Royal College of Art in London. In 1977 he moved to Germany and taught at the Kunstakademie Düsseldorf. The following year he had his first solo exhibitions, at the Lisson Gallery in London, Lutzowstrasse Situation in Berlin, and Kunstlerhaus Weidenallee in Hamburg. At a time in which Minimalism, Conceptual art, and Arte Povera were dominant, Cragg came to be considered one of the leading figures of the renewal of sculpture. Like Carl Andre, Richard Long, and Bruce Nauman, among others, Cragg extended the realm of sculpture by introducing new materials; his first sculpture was made of plastic, for example, and he also included found objects and various raw materials in his work. In doing so, Cragg attempted to adapt the components of his work to the world around him. He differentiated between art conceived in a certain ideal framework—like the work of Constantin Brancusi, Alberto Giacometti, and Andy Warhol—and art created by instinct in relation to the world, like that of Edgar Degas, Medardo Rosso, and Joseph Beuys. In the 1980s Cragg's work became influenced by scientists and philosophers such as Isaac Newton and Alain Prochiantz. He began to create wood sculptures whose forms are reminiscent of the domestic architecture of the Norwegian fjords region and giant versions of laboratory equipment.

Cragg participated in Documenta in Kassel in 1982 and 1987, and represented England at the Venice Biennale in 1988, the same year he received the Turner Prize. In 1994 he was elected to the Royal Academy. Cragg lives and works in Wuppertal, Germany.

WILLEM DE KOONING

Willem de Kooning was born in 1904 in Rotterdam. From 1916 to 1925 he studied at night at the Academie van Beeldende Kunsten en Technische Wetenschappen in Rotterdam while apprenticed to a commercial-art and decorating firm and later working for an art director. In 1924 he visited museums in Belgium and studied further in Brussels and Antwerp. De Kooning moved to the United States in 1926 and the following year settled in New York, where he met Stuart Davis, Arshile Gorky, and John Graham. He took various commercial-art and odd jobs until 1935–36, when he was employed in the mural and easel divisions of the Works Progress Administration's Federal Art Project. Thereafter he painted full-time. During the 1930s his work had a great affinity with that of his friends John Graham and Arshile Gorky and evinced the influence of Pablo Picasso and Joan Miró.

In 1938 de Kooning started his first series of *Women*, which would become a major recurrent theme. During the 1940s he participated in group shows with other artists who would form the New York School. De Kooning's first solo show, which took place at the Egan Gallery in New York in 1948, established his reputation as a major artist; it included a number of the allover black-and-white abstractions he had initiated in 1946. The *Women* of the early 1950s were followed by abstract urban landscapes, *Parkways*, rural landscapes, and, in the 1960s, a new group of *Women*.

In 1968 de Kooning visited the Netherlands for the first time since 1926, for the opening of his retrospective at the Stedelijk Museum in Amsterdam. In Rome in 1969 he executed his first sculptures—figures modeled in clay and later cast in bronze—and in 1970–71 he began a series of life-size figures. In 1974 the Walker Art Center in Minneapolis organized a show of de Kooning's drawings and sculpture that traveled throughout the United States, and in 1978 the Solomon R. Guggenheim Museum in New York mounted an exhibition of his recent work. In 1979 de Kooning and Eduardo Chillida received the Andrew W. Mellon Prize, which was accompanied by an exhibition at the Museum of Art of the Carnegie Institute in Pittsburgh. In 1963 de Kooning settled in East Hampton, Long Island, where he died in 1997.

RICHARD DIEBENKORN

Richard Diebenkorn was born in 1922 in Portland, Oregon. He spent his childhood in San Francisco and entered Stanford University in 1940, where he studied fine arts and art history under the direction of Victor Arnautoff and Daniel Mendelowitz. He was interested in American artists such as Arthur Dove, Edward Hopper, and Charles Sheeler, but also European artists like Paul Cézanne, Henri Matisse, and Pablo Picasso. During World War II, Diebenkorn enlisted in the Marines, and the locations of his postings allowed him to visit important collections of modern art in Europe. In this way he formed an international style, absorbing diverse influences, from Paul Klee and Joan Miró to Julio González, Kurt Schwitters, and Mark Rothko, evident in the abstract watercolor paintings he made at this time.

In 1946 Diebenkorn returned to San Francisco and studied at the California School of Fine Arts (now San Francisco Art Institute), where he met contemporaries such as David Park, who would become a major influence. While on scholarship for a year in New York, he met William Baziotes and Bradley Walker Tomlin, whose influence, along with that of Picasso, was also decisive at this time. After returning to San Francisco, Diebenkorn taught at the California School of Fine Arts, alongside Park and Edward Corbett. His so-called Sausalito period took shape during these years, and other periods would follow, mostly taking the name of the city in which they were realized: the Albuquerque period (1950–52, his first mature period), Urban period (1952–53), and Berkeley period (1953–55). Diebenkorn then broke with abstraction, depicting landscapes, figures, and still lifes. This lasted until 1965, when he began a new figurative cycle. With the 1967 work *Ocean Park*, he returned definitively to abstraction and a pictorial language that developed through the end of his life.

Diebenkorn had his first show in 1948 at the California Palace of the Legion of Honor, San Francisco. In 1956 he participated in the first show of the Group of Nine at the Poindexter Gallery in New York. The first important retrospective of his work took place at the Albright-Knox Art Gallery in Buffalo, New York, in 1976–77; the show then traveled to Washington, D.C., Cincinnati, Los Angeles, and Oakland. In 1989 John Elderfield, a curator at the Museum of Modern Art, New York, organized a show of Diebenkorn's works on paper, which constituted an important part of his production. Diebenkorn died in 1993 in Berkeley, California.

MARK DI SUVERO

Mark di Suvero was born in 1933 in Shanghai. In 1941 he moved with his family to San Francisco. From 1954 to 1956 he attended the University of California, first in Santa Barbara and then in Berkeley, during which time he began painting and sculpting. In 1957 he moved to New York, where he discovered Abstract Expressionism, joined the cooperative March Gallery, and exhibited pieces in plaster and wax. In 1959 he began to make sculptures out of wood from demolished buildings. The following year, while working in construction to support himself financially, he was involved in a serious jobsite accident that left him critically injured. In 1963 he was a founding member of the Park Place Gallery.

In 1964 di Suvero made his first outdoor sculpture. Three years later, after learning how to use a crane, lifting platform, torch, and welder, he created his first large outdoor crane-assisted all-steel piece, *Are Years What? (for Marianne Moore)*. In 1971 he left the United States for Europe due to his opposition to the Vietnam War. He had a solo exhibition at the Stedelijk Van Abbemuseum and in gardens around the city of Eindoven the following year, and in 1975 he was the first living artist to exhibit in the Jardin des Tuileries in Paris. With peace in Vietnam that year, di Suvero returned to the United States.

On his return, the Whitney Museum of American Art in New York held a retrospective of his work, which was installed throughout the city. In 1977 he founded the Athena Foundation, an association that helps artists to create monumental sculpture, and Socrates Sculpture Park in Long Island City, New York. Di Suvero received the Lifetime Achievement in Contemporary Sculpture Award from the International Sculpture Center in 2000, and in 2005 he was presented with the Heinz Award in the Arts and Humanities. Di Suvero lives and works in New York; Petaluma, California; and Chalon-sur-Saône, France.

JEAN DUBUFFET

Jean Dubuffet was born in 1901 in Le Havre, France. He attended art classes in his youth and in 1918 moved to Paris to study at the Académie Julian, which he left after six months. During this time Dubuffet met Raoul Dufy, Max Jacob, Fernand Léger, and Suzanne Valadon and became fascinated with Hans Prinzhorn's book on psychopathic art. He traveled to Italy in 1923 and South America in 1924. Dubuffet then gave up painting for about ten years, working as an industrial draftsman and later in the family wine business. He committed himself to becoming an artist in 1942.

Dubuffet's first solo exhibition was held at the Galerie René Drouin in Paris in 1944. During the 1940s the artist associated with André Breton, Georges Limbour, Jean Paulhan, and Charles Ratton. His style and subject matter in this period owed a debt to Paul Klee. From 1945 he collected Art Brut, spontaneous, direct works by untutored individuals such as mental patients. The Pierre Matisse Gallery gave him his first solo show in New York in 1947.

From 1951 to 1952 Dubuffet lived in New York. He then returned to Paris, where a retrospective of his work took place at the Cercle Volney in 1954. His first museum retrospective occurred in 1957 at the Schloss Morsbroich in Leverkusen. Dubuffet exhibitions were subsequently held at the Musée des Arts Décoratifs, Paris, in 1960–61; the Museum of Modern Art, New York, and Art Institute of Chicago in 1962; Palazzo Grassi, Venice, in 1964; Tate Gallery, London, and Stedelijk Museum, Amsterdam, in 1966; and Solomon R. Guggenheim Museum, New York, in 1966–67. A collection of Dubuffet's writings, *Prospectus et tous écrits suivants*, was published in 1967, the same year he started making architectural structures. Soon thereafter he began numerous commissions for monumental outdoor sculptures. In 1971 he produced his first theater props, the "practicables." A Dubuffet retrospective was presented at the Akademie der Kunst, Berlin, the Museum Moderner Kunst, Vienna, and the Joseph-Haubrichkunsthalle, Cologne, in 1980–81. In 1981 the Solomon R. Guggenheim Museum observed the artist's eightieth birthday with an exhibition. Dubuffet died in 1985 in Paris.

PERICLE FAZZINI

Pericle Fazzini was born in 1913 in Grottammare, Italy. He made his first sculptures in the studio of his father, a wood-carver. In 1929, at the insistence of family friend and poet Mario Rivosecchi, Fazzini's father sent him to Rome, where he took drawing classes at the Accademia di Belle Arti. In 1931 he won a competition for his design for the tomb for Cardinal Dusmet in Catania, Italy, and a year later he won the Pensionato Artistico Nazionale, which provided him with the funds necessary to rent a studio in Rome for the next three years. From 1937 to 1952 he served as an instructor at the Museo Artistico Industriale in Rome. During this period he explored different materials in his sculpture, including clay and bronze, won the Premio dell'Accademia d'Italia (in 1942), and had his first solo exhibition (at the Galleria La Margherita, Rome, in 1943) and retrospective (at the Palazzo Barberini, Rome, in 1951). He continued to teach through most of the 1950s, first at the Accademia di Belle Arti in Florence and then at the Accademia di Brera in Milan.

Fazzini's earliest works were mostly relief sculptures carved in wood: Baroque-inspired compositions with an emphasis on movement and plasticity, such as *The Dance* (*La danza*, 1933–35). Over the next decade his style would take on a more sober affect, though he would never relinquish his preoccupation with plasticity and the idea of the "unfinished" as a means of heightening a work's expressive quality. In the late 1930s and early 1940s he began to focus more attention on portraiture subtly infused with a sense of humanity; Fazzini's portrait of Giuseppe Ungaretti from 1936 inspired the poet to call him "a sculptor of the wind." The artist returned to a more Baroque sensibility in the period between 1946 and 1955 with works in which he combined figures from real life and fantasy with a sense of dynamic visual rhythm.

Fazzini is best known for his later, more monumental works, including *Monument to the Resistance* (*Monumento alla Resistenza*, 1956) in Ancona and *Resurrection* (*La resurrezione*, 1972–77), commissioned by the Vatican for one of its main halls. The latter work, a sixty-six-foot-tall sculpture in bronze and brass, depicts Christ emerging from the aftermath of a nuclear explosion, and was unveiled by Pope Paul VI in 1977. Fazzini died in Rome in 1987.

LUCIO FONTANA

Lucio Fontana was born in 1899 in Rosario de Santa Fé, Argentina, to an Italian father and Argentinean mother. He lived in Milan from 1905 to 1922 and then moved back to Argentina, where he worked as a sculptor in his father's studio for several years before opening his own. In 1926 he participated in the first exhibition of Nexus, a group of young Argentinean artists working in Rosario de Santa Fé. Upon his return to Milan in 1928, Fontana enrolled at the Accademia di Belle Arti di Brera, which he attended for two years.

The Galleria del Milione, Milan, presented Fontana's first solo exhibition in 1930. The artist traveled to Paris in 1935 and joined the Abstraction-Création group there. The same year, he developed his skills in ceramics in Albisola, Italy, and later at the Sèvres factory, near Paris. In 1939 he joined the Corrente, a group of expressionist artists in Milan. He moved to Buenos Aires the following year. In 1946, with some of his students, he founded the Academia de Altamira, from which emerged the Manifiesto Blanco group. Fontana moved back to Milan in 1947 and, in collaboration with a group of writers and philosophers, signed the *Primo manifesto dello Spazialismo*.

The year 1949 marked a turning point in Fontana's career; he concurrently created the *Buchi* ("holes"), his first series of paintings in which he punctured the canvas, and his first spatial environment, a combination of shapeless sculptures, fluorescent paintings, and black lights to be viewed in a dark room. The latter work soon led him to employ neon tubing in ceiling decorations. In the early 1950s he participated in Italian exhibitions of Art Informel. During this decade he explored various effects, such as slashing and perforating, in both painting and sculpture. The artist visited New York in 1961 during a show of his work at the Martha Jackson Gallery. In 1966 he designed opera sets and costumes for La Scala in Milan. In the last year of his career, Fontana became increasingly interested in the staging of his work in the many exhibitions that honored him worldwide, as well as in the idea of purity, which informed his last white canvases. These concerns were prominent at the 1966 Venice Biennale, for which he designed the environment for his work, and at the 1968 Documenta in Kassel. Fontana died in 1968 in Comabbio, Italy.

SAM FRANCIS

Sam Francis was born in San Mateo, California, in 1923. He joined the U.S. Air Force in 1943, after studying medicine and psychology at the University of California, Berkeley, but started painting as a form of therapy after a plane accident left him hospitalized for an extended period. From 1945 to 1946 he studied painting at the California School of Fine Arts (now San Francisco Art Institute) in San Francisco, and in 1947 produced his first abstract composition. He spent the following two years studying art history at the University of California, Berkeley, and graduated with an MA in literary studies.

In 1950 Francis moved to Paris and two years later had his first solo exhibition at the Galerie du Dragon. At that time his style was deeply affected by Art Informel and by the Abstract Expressionist works of Jackson Pollock. In 1955 he participated in his first museum exhibition, presenting seven paintings at *Tendances actuelles* at the Kunsthalle Bern. The following year he took part in the exhibition *Twelve Americans* at the Museum of Modern Art in New York. In 1957 he spent some time in Mexico, New York, and Japan. His visit to Japan had a significant impact on his artistic development, and this is clearly seen in his work of the time, characterized by techniques associated with Japanese art, such as the use of thin layers of paint and large blank areas of canvas.

In 1959 Francis took part in Documenta in Kassel and the São Paulo Bienal. In 1961, despite falling ill and spending a long time in a hospital in Bern, he participated in the exhibitions *Arte e contemplazione* at the Palazzo Grassi in Venice and *Abstract Expressionists and Imaginists* at the Solomon R. Guggenheim Museum in New York. Though known primarily as a painter, he was also a sculptor and printmaker, and produced a new series of color lithographs in 1963. In 1984 he founded the Lapis Press, a publishing house specializing in visual arts and philosophy. His work is held by many public and private collections, including the Museum of Modern Art, New York; Musée National d'Art Moderne, Centre Pompidou, Paris; and Idemitsu Museum of Art, Tokyo. Francis died in 1994 in Santa Monica, California.

ADOLPH GOTTLIEB

Adolph Gottlieb was born in New York in 1903. In 1920 he left high school and enrolled in the Art Students League, where he studied under Robert Henri and John Sloan. The following year he left for Europe, where he spent six months studying at the Académie de la Grande Chaumière in Paris and another year traveling throughout Germany and Central Europe. On his return to the United States, he attended Parsons School of Design and the Cooper Union in New York. During the 1930s he worked as a teacher.

In 1935 Gottlieb founded a group called The Ten, along with artists such as William Baziotes, Ilya Bolotowsky, Lee Gatch, and Mark Rothko. His early works were representational paintings of American scenes, but after he spent eight months in Arizona in 1937, his work became more surrealistic, as in *The Sea Chest* (1942), and he began to create monumental paintings in which the desert landscape forms the background. In 1941 Gottlieb began to work on his *Pictographs*, presenting them the following

year in an exhibition at the Wildenstein Galleries in New York. In 1943 he and Mark Rothko, leading figures of the New York School, wrote a letter to the *New York Times* in which they explained the theoretical principles of Abstract Expressionism. At the beginning of the 1950s, he started the *Imaginary Landscapes* series. This was followed, in 1956, by the *Bursts* series, which featured simplified images, as in *Blast I* (1957). In the 1960s he employed similar forms in sculptures such as *Petaloid* (1967).

In 1946 Gottlieb's work was included in the *Exposition internationale d'art moderne* at the Musée National d'Art Moderne in Paris. The following year his work was included in the exhibition *La peinture moderne américaine* at Galerie Maeght in Paris. In 1963 he won the Grand Prize at the São Paulo Bienal. The first retrospective of his work, co-organized by the Whitney Museum of American Art and the Solomon R. Guggenheim Museum in New York, took place in 1968. Having suffered a stroke that left him partially paralyzed in 1970, Gottlieb died in 1974 in New York.

PHILIP GUSTON

Philip Guston was born in Montreal in 1913, but grew up in Los Angeles. He began to paint in 1927, and in 1930 attended the Otis Art Institute in Los Angeles for a few months. Interested in the work of Giorgio de Chirico and the masters of the Italian Renaissance, especially Piero della Francesca, Andrea Mantegna, and Paolo Ucello, he attempted to integrate aspects of this model with the more recent developments of pictorial Cubism in his work of the 1930s. During this period he also paid attention to the mural paintings of Mexican artists such as Diego Rivera. His work developed in New York after he moved there in 1935. Employed by the Works Progress Administration's Federal Art Project, he worked on murals at the WPA Building at the World's Fair (*Maintaining America's Skills*, 1939) and the Queensbridge Housing Project (1940) in New York, and at the Social Security Building in Washington, D.C. (1942). In the 1940s Guston returned to easel painting, developing a style that drew on mythology, as in the paintings *Martial Memory* (1945) and *If This Be Not I* (1945). In the late 1940s he painted in an increasingly abstract style, doing away with figures altogether, as in the painting *The Tormentors* (1947–48). In the 1950s his work became entirely abstract. It changed again in the 1960s, when he developed a new figurative style, as seen in *Evidence* (1970).

The first major exhibition of Guston's work was held at the State University of Iowa in Iowa City in 1944. He received a John Simon Guggenheim Memorial Foundation fellowship in 1947 and in 1959 was awarded a Ford Foundation grant. He taught at New York University from 1951 to 1958 and Pratt Institute from 1953 to 1958. In 1967 he moved to Woodstock, New York, where he died in 1980.

HANS HARTUNG

Hans Hartung was born in 1904 in Leipzig, Germany. He studied philosophy and art history at the Akademie der Bildenden Künste in Leipzig and then in Dresden, after which he moved to Monaco to study under the painter Max Doerner. In 1932 Hartung went to Paris, where he met Alexander Calder, Vasily Kandinsky, Joan Miró, and Piet Mondrian, and showed his first works at the Salon des Indépendants. During World War II, Hartung joined the French Foreign Legion, returning to Paris after the war to become a French citizen. After six years of inactivity as an artist, he began painting again and participated in numerous group exhibitions, showing works characterized by large colored stripes overpainted with calligraphic lines. During the 1960s he began to introduce three-dimensional elements into his paintings.

In 1947 Hartung had his first solo exhibition, the opening show of Galerie Lydia Conti in Paris. Between 1955 and 1964 he participated several times in Documenta in Kassel. He received the Guggenheim International Prize in 1956 and the Grand Prize for Painting at the Venice Biennale in 1960. In 1976 he published his memoirs under the title *Autoportrait*. The following year he was elected a member of the Académie des Beaux-Arts in Paris. Also in 1977 Hartung had his first exhibition of photographs at Cercle Noroit in Arras, and the Centre Georges Pompidou organized an exhibition of his lithographs and etchings that traveled around France for four years. In 1981 the Städtische Kunsthalle Düsseldorf, Staatsgalerie Moderner Kunst in Munich, and Henie-Onstad Foundation in Oslo presented a major retrospective exhibition following his receipt of the first annual Oskar Kokoschka Prize from the Austrian government. In 1985 the Grand Palais in Paris presented a major retrospective of his work. Hartung died in 1989 in Antibes, France.

BARBARA HEPWORTH

Barbara Hepworth was born in 1903 in Wakefield, England. She studied sculpture at the Leeds School of Art and the Royal College of Art in London from 1920 to 1924. In September 1924 she traveled to Italy, settling in Rome, where she began her career as a sculptor. In 1926 she returned to London, moving to 7 The Mall Studios in Hampstead in 1928. In 1931 she joined the London Group and the 7 & 5 Society. In 1931 Hepworth met Ben Nicholson, whom she would marry in 1938.

Hepworth's sculpture became increasingly abstract from 1932 on. She and Nicholson became involved in the group Abstraction-Création in 1933 and in Paul Nash's group Unit One the following year. After a break from sculpting starting in 1939, she returned with a new interest in hollowing precise shapes out of her sculpted material (stone or wood), which permitted her to play with the interior and exterior of the same sculpture. An interest in Constructivism led to publication of the book *Circle: International Survey of Constructive Art*, edited by Nicholson, Naum Gabo, and Leslie Martin and designed by Hepworth and Sadie Martin, in 1937. At the outbreak of World War II, Hepworth moved to St Ives in Cornwall, where she formed the Penwith Society of Arts with Nicholson, Peter Lanyon, and others.

The first major exhibition of Hepworth's work was presented in 1943 at Temple Newsam in Leeds. In the 1950s several institutions held touring retrospectives of her work, including the Wakefield City Art Gallery in 1951, Whitechapel Gallery, London, in 1954, and Walker Art Center, Minneapolis, in 1955. She won the Grand Prize at the São Paulo Bienal in 1959. In 1964 the British Council organized an exhibition of her work that toured Europe, and the same year her sculpture *Single Form* (1961–64) was erected in front of the United Nations building in New York. Alan Bowness published the catalogue raisonné of her work in 1971. Hepworth died in St Ives in 1975. Following her death, her house and studio became a museum dedicated to her work.

HANS HOFMANN

Hans Hofmann was born in 1880 in Weissenburg, Bavaria. He was raised in Munich, where in 1898 he began to study at various art schools. The patronage of Philip Freudenberg, a Berlin art collector, enabled Hofmann to live in Paris from 1904 to 1914. In Paris he attended the Académie Colarossi and the Académie de la Grande Chaumière; he met Georges Braque, Pablo Picasso, and other Cubists and was a friend of Robert Delaunay, who stimulated his interest in color. In 1909 Hofmann exhibited with the Neue Sezession in Berlin, and in 1910 was given his first solo exhibition at the Galerie Paul Cassirer there. During this period he painted in a Cubist style.

At the outbreak of World War I, Hofmann was in Munich; disqualified from military service due to a lung condition, he remained there and in 1915 opened an art school, which became highly successful. The artist taught at the University of California at Berkeley during the summer of 1930. He returned to teach in California in 1931, and his first exhibition in the United States took place that summer at the California Palace of the Legion of Honor in San Francisco. In 1932 he closed his Munich school and decided to settled in the United States. His first school in New York opened in 1933 and was succeeded in 1934 by the Hans Hofmann School of Fine Arts, also in New York; in 1935 he established a summer school in Provincetown, Massachusetts.

After an extended period devoted to drawing, Hofmann returned to painting in 1935, combining Cubist structure, vivid color, and emphatic gesture. He became a U.S. citizen in 1941. By the 1940s his work had become completely abstract. Hofmann's first solo exhibition in New York took place at Peggy Guggenheim's gallery Art of This Century in 1944. In 1958 he closed his schools to devote himself full-time to painting. Hofmann died in 1966 in New York.

JENNY HOLZER

Jenny Holzer was born in 1950 in Gallipolis, Ohio. She graduated with a degree in painting and printmaking from Ohio University in 1972 and started an MFA program at the Rhode Island School of Design in Providence in 1975. During this period she began integrating written words and language into her work. She received her MFA in 1977 and moved to New York, where she enrolled in the Whitney Museum of American Art's Independent Study Program. It was there that she commenced her *Truisms* series, her first works comprising text alone. She had the words printed on sheets of paper, which she either distributed as fliers or posted anonymously around the city.

Holzer's work reformulates the assumptions of traditional forms of art, especially in the context of public space. Writing is still the basis of her creative process, whether it is used alone or in combination with other modes of representation, ranging from installations to xenon projections. Her texts have appeared on electronic signs; printed on posters and T-shirts; engraved on stone benches, floors, and sarcophagi; and cast on bronze and silver plaques. Her words have also appeared on billboards, in newspapers, and on the Internet and have been projected onto the facades of buildings, hillsides, and liquid surfaces via laser and xenon projections.

Holzer's projects have been presented at museums all over the world, including the Solomon R. Guggenheim Museum, New York (1989), Centre Pompidou, Paris (1996), the Museum of Modern Art, New York (1997), Whitney Museum of American Art, New York (1999), Museet for Samtidskunst, Oslo (2000), and Neue Nationalgalerie, Berlin (2001). In 1990 she was invited to show at the Venice Biennale and was awarded the Golden Lion for the best national pavilion. She received the Crystal Award from the World Economic Forum in 1996 and the Berlin Prize Fellowship from the Berlin American Academy in 2000. Holzer lives and works in Hoosick, New York.

JASPER JOHNS

Jasper Johns was born in 1930 in Augusta, Georgia, and grew up in South Carolina. He studied at the University of South Carolina in Columbia from 1947 to 1948, before moving to New York. In the mid-1950s Johns began to paint a series of works depicting the American flag, developing this work into a style that became increasingly complex. In 1958 the Leo Castelli Gallery in New York presented Johns's first solo show, from which the Museum of Modern Art acquired three works. His work of this period was considered both a continuation of and an attack against Abstract Expressionism, but at the end of the 1950s his style changed as he began to focus increasingly on process. In 1961 he introduced a map of the United States as a motif in his work. During the decade that followed, Johns made his first gray monochromatic paintings; experimentation with monochromatic painting would remain a preoccupation throughout his career. In the 1980s he again introduced new motifs into his work, including popular icons, images, and patterns he saw in his everyday life, and Matthias Grünewald's Isenheim Altarpiece. In the late 1980s Johns would reference Pablo Picasso in several of his works; the *Four Seasons*

series of 1986, for example, quotes Picasso's *The Shadow* (*L'ombre*, 1953).

In 1964 a large retrospective of Johns's work was presented at the Jewish Museum in New York and traveled to the Whitechapel Gallery in London. He participated in the Venice Biennale the same year. In 1965 he had a retrospective at the Pasadena Art Museum in Pasadena, California, and received a prize at the International Biennial of Graphic Art in Ljubljana, in the former Yugoslavia. In 1977 the Whitney Museum of American Art in New York organized a retrospective that traveled to the Kunsthalle Köln in Cologne, Musée National d'Art Moderne in Paris, Hayward Gallery in London, Seibu Museum of Art in Tokyo, and San Francisco Museum of Art. In 1988 he was awarded the Grand Prize for Painting at the Venice Biennale. Johns lives and works in Sharon, Connecticut.

DONALD JUDD

Donald Judd was born in 1928 in Excelsior Springs, Missouri. He registered at the Art Students League in New York in 1948 but transferred a few months later to the College of William and Mary in Williamsburg, Virginia. In 1949 he moved back to New York to study philosophy at Columbia University while he took art classes at the Art Students League.

The Panoramas Gallery organized his first solo exhibition in 1957. That same year Judd took art history classes at Columbia University. He began to write articles for *Art News* in 1959 and the next year became a contributing editor for *Arts Magazine*. In 1965 he started writing reviews for *Art International*. In the early 1960s he switched from painting to sculpture and started to develop an interest in architecture. Judd challenged the artistic convention of originality by using industrial processes and materials—such as steel, concrete, and plywood—to create large, hollow Minimalist sculptures, mostly in the form of boxes, which he arranged in repeated simple geometric forms.

His second solo show was held at the Green Gallery in New York in 1963. From 1962 to 1964 he worked as an instructor at the Brooklyn Institute of Arts and Sciences. The Leo Castelli Gallery in New York organized the first of a long series of individual exhibitions in 1966. That year Judd was also hired as a visiting artist at Dartmouth College in Hanover, New Hampshire, and the following year he taught sculpture at Yale University in New Haven. The Whitney Museum of American Art in New York organized the first retrospective of his work in 1968. The artist received many fellowships during the 1960s, among them a grant from the John Simon Guggenheim Memorial Foundation in 1968.

In 1971 he participated in the Guggenheim International Award exhibition at the Solomon R. Guggenheim Museum in New York, along with other Minimalist and Conceptual artists. Judd moved to Marfa, Texas, in 1972. He participated in his first Venice Biennale in 1980, and in Documenta in Kassel in 1982. In 1984 he started designing furniture. During the first half of the 1980s, Judd worked on plans for the Chinati Foundation in Marfa; the renovated compound of buildings opened in 1986 as a showcase for his sculptures, as well as for the work of other contemporary artists.

In 1987 Judd was honored by a large exhibition at the Stedelijk Van Abbemuseum in Eindhoven; this show traveled to Düsseldorf, Paris, Barcelona, and Turin. The Whitney Museum of American Art organized a traveling retrospective of his work in 1988. In 1992 he was elected a member of the Royal Academy of Fine Arts in Stockholm and received a prize from the Stankowski Foundation in Stuttgart, increasing the list of his numerous awards. During his lifetime Judd published a large body of theoretical writings, in which he rigorously promoted the cause of Minimalist art; these essays were consolidated in two volumes published in 1975 and 1987. The artist died in 1994 in New York.

ANISH KAPOOR

Anish Kapoor was born in 1954 in Bombay (now Mumbai), India. He moved to England when he was nineteen years old to attend the Hornsey College of Art in London (1973–77), followed by the Chelsea School of Art (1977–78). Upon concluding his studies, he taught at Wolverhampton Polytechnic in 1979. The following year Kapoor had his first solo show, at the studio of Patrice Alexandre in Paris. In the early 1980s he was one of the principal artists associated with New British Sculpture, a term applied also to the work of Tony Cragg and Anthony Gormley, among others. Kapoor's sculptural oeuvre at this time revolved around a multiplicity of new forms that created dialogue between two- and three-dimensionality.

Throughout the 1980s, Kapoor continued this investigation of oppositions in sculptures that were partially abstract and completely coated in pure pigment. In the 1990s his works assumed an increasingly monumental scale and were often centered on the idea of the void. In 1990 Kapoor represented Great Britain at the Venice Biennale, where he won the Premio Duemila, and the following year he was the recipient of the Turner Prize.

Among Kapoor's numerous private and public commissions is *Cloud Gate*, an enormous elliptical arc made of reflective stainless steel, unveiled in Millennium Park in Chicago in 2004. Kapoor is said to have derived his inspiration for the piece from liquid mercury. Significant exhibitions of his work have been held at the Hayward Gallery in London (1998), Museo Archeologico Nazionale in Naples (2003), and the Royal Academy of Arts in London and Guggenheim Museum Bilbao (2009–10). Kapoor lives and works in London.

ELLSWORTH KELLY

Ellsworth Kelly was born in 1923 in Newburgh, New York. He studied at the Pratt Institute in Brooklyn from 1941 to 1943. After military service from 1943 to 1945, he attended the School of the Museum of Fine Arts in Boston from 1946 to 1948. The following year Kelly went to France and enrolled at the École des Beaux-Arts in Paris under the GI Bill, although he attended classes infrequently. In France he discovered Romanesque art and architecture and Byzantine art. He was also introduced to Surrealism and Neo-Plasticism, which led him to experiment with automatic drawing and geometric abstraction.

Kelly abstracts the forms in his paintings from observations of the real world, such as shadows cast by trees or the spaces between architectural elements. In 1950 Kelly met Jean Arp and that same year began to make shaped-wood reliefs and collages in which he arranged the elements according to the laws of chance. He soon began to make paintings in separate panels that could be recombined to produce different compositions, as well as multipanel paintings in which each canvas was painted a single color. During the 1950s he traveled throughout France, where he met Constantin Brancusi, Alexander Calder, Alberto Magnelli, Francis Picabia, and Georges Vantongerloo, among other artists. His first solo show took place at the Galerie Arnaud Lefebvre, Paris, in 1951.

Kelly returned to the United States in 1954, living first in a studio apartment on Broad Street, New York, and then at Coenties Slip in lower Manhattan, where his neighbors would through the years include Robert Indiana, Agnes Martin, Fred Mitchell, James Rosenquist, Lenore Tawney, and Jack Youngerman. His first solo show in New York was held at the Betty Parsons Gallery in 1956, and three years later he was included in *Sixteen Americans* at the Museum of Modern Art, New York. In 1958 he also began to make freestanding sculptures. He moved out of Manhattan in 1970, setting up a studio in Chatham and a home in nearby Spencertown, New York, where he currently lives and works.

Kelly's first retrospective was held at the Museum of Modern Art, New York, in 1973. The following year Kelly began an ongoing series of totemic sculptures in steel and aluminum. He traveled throughout Spain, Italy, and France in 1977, when his work was included in Documenta in Kassel. He has executed many public commissions, including a mural for UNESCO in Paris in 1969, a sculpture for the city of Barcelona in 1978, and a memorial for the United States Holocaust Memorial Museum in Washington, D.C., in 1993. Kelly has received numerous retrospective exhibitions, including a sculpture exhibition at the Whitney Museum of American Art in New York in 1982; an exhibition of works on paper and print works that traveled extensively in the United States and Canada from 1987 to 1988; and a career retrospective in 1996 organized by the Solomon R. Guggenheim Museum in New York, which traveled to the Museum of Contemporary Art in Los Angeles, Tate Gallery in London, and Haus der Kunst in Munich. Since then solo exhibitions of Kelly's work have been mounted at the Metropolitan Museum of Art in New York (1998), Fogg Art Museum at Harvard University in Cambridge, Massachusetts (1999), San Francisco Museum of Modern Art (2002), Philadelphia Museum of Art (2007), and Museum of Modern Art in New York (2007).